Praise for *From Cataloguing to Metadata Cr*

'*From Cataloguing to Metadata Creation* is a: theoretical and methodological basis for the creation of metadata, an activity fully embedded in the scientific and disciplinary field of cataloguing.

It charts the evolution of cataloguing in the modern world, up to and including the intersection with the methodologies of the Semantic Web and linked open data. In this environment the "relationship" between the described entities is not only pushed to its own maximum potential within a (bibliographic) catalogue, but also multiplies its information potential. Indeed, it projects itself into the web of data, where there are extraordinary opportunities to create and share further cultural production.'
Rosa Maiello, President, Italian Library Association

From Cataloguing to
Metadata Creation

From Cataloguing to Metadata Creation

A Cultural and Methodological Introduction

Mauro Guerrini

Prefaces by Barbara B. Tillett and Peter Lor
Afterword by Giovanni Bergamin

fp facet
publishing

© Mauro Guerrini 2023

Published by Facet Publishing
c/o British Library, 96 Euston Road, London NW1 2DB
www.facetpublishing.co.uk

Facet Publishing is wholly owned by CILIP: the Library and Information Association.

The author has asserted his right under the Copyright, Designs and Patents Act 1988 to be identified as author of this work.

Every effort has been made to contact the holders of copyright material reproduced in this text, and thanks are due to them for permission to reproduce the material indicated. If there are any queries please contact the publisher.

British Library Cataloguing in Publication Data
A catalogue record for this book is available from the British Library.

ISBN 978-1-78330-628-2 (paperback)
ISBN 978-1-78330-629-9 (hardback)
ISBN 978-1-78330-630-5 (PDF)
ISBN 978-1-78330-631-2 (EPUB)

First published 2023
Originally published in Italian as *Dalla catalogazione alla metadatazione: Tracce di un percorso.*

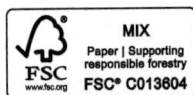

MIX
Paper | Supporting responsible forestry
FSC
www.fsc.org   FSC® C013604

The manufacturer's authorised representative in the EU for product safety is Logos Europe, 9 rue Nicolas Poussin, 17000 La Rochelle, France (contact@logoseurope.eu, www.logoseurope.eu).

Typeset from author's files in 10.5/13 pt Revival 565 and Frutiger by Flagholme Publishing Services.
Printed and made in Great Britain by CPI Group (UK) Ltd, Croydon, CR0 4YY.

To Leonida, *my grandson*

New technologies will always underpin future generations of library catalogues. In order to maintain their role in providing information, serving users, and fulfilling their mission as cultural heritage and memory institutions, libraries must take a technological leap for the next generation; library bibliographic standards, models, and services, must be transformed to those of the Semantic Web.

Gordon Dunsire, Mirna Willer,
Bibliographic Information Organization in the Semantic Web

It is incumbent on us to 'listen to the colour of our dreams'. If we are not clear about our core values, no-one else can be expected to understand the purpose of what we do. There are grounds for optimism.

Alan Danskin,
https://archive.ifla.org/IV/ifla72/papers/102-Danskin-en.pdf

An excellent librarian – this is what catalogers are and will continue to be in the future.

Michael A. Cerbo,
Is there a future for library catalogers?,
Cataloging & Classification Quarterly

Contents

Figures

About the Author

Mauro Guerrini is Professor of Library Science, Cataloguing, Metadata Creation and Classification, and Dean of the Masters on Cataloguing and Metadata Creation of Manuscript, Printed and Digital Resources at the University of Florence, Italy. He obtained the Diploma of Librarianship and the Diploma in the Conservation of Manuscripts at the School for Archivists and Librarians at the University of Rome La Sapienza, and later gained the Archivist's Certificate from the State Archive in Florence. Mauro is author of numerous publications on cataloguing, ethics, open access and the history of librarians, in particular Antonio Panizzi. He is a member of the editorial board of *Cataloging & Classification Quarterly, AIB Studi, Biblioteche Oggi*, and other journals, and Chair of the series *Libraries and Librarians* (Florence University Press); he is also Founder and Editor in Chief of *JLIS.it: Italian Journal of Library and Information Science*.

Mauro has been a Fellow of AIB (Italian Library Association) since 1979, AIB President (2005–11), Fellow of ABEI, SISBB, and member of other organisations. He was Chair of the AIB Section on Cataloguing, member of the IFLA ISBD Review Group, IFLA Cataloguing Section, Subject Analysis and Bibliography Sections. He was President of the Italian National Committee of IFLA Congress 2009, Chair of the 2021 International Conference on Electronic Resources, 2003 International Conference on Authority Control, 2012 Global Interoperability and Linked Data in Libraries and 2022 International Conference Bibliographic Control in the Digital Ecosystem.

Prefaces

by Barbara B. Tillett and Peter Lor

Cataloguing standards, rules and guidelines have changed through the ages from individual instructions for individual libraries to now internationally shared guidance built for the international exchange of bibliographic data. This work by Professor Guerrini provides an overview of the changes that have taken place in cataloguing standards and the great work of shared standards of international organisations, primarily the International Federation of Library Associations and Institutions (IFLA), towards reaching that ideal of 'universal bibliographic control'. Even universal bibliographic control is a concept that continues to evolve as the capabilities for documenting and sharing bibliographic data evolve.

At first, our technologies only allowed individual libraries to build their catalogues. Afterwards, the idea of creating copies of that cataloguing, such as in a book catalogue, emerged as printing developed. Technology advanced to enable printing catalogue cards to purchase from a centralised source when a library added holdings held by another library. We moved through several phases of automation from being able at first to exchange records in a standard format to later re-using data available internationally on the web or simply to link to existing data, wherever it resides.

Cataloguing is a costly operation, so the idea to share as much of that work as we can emerged early on. To share, we all need to use the same standards and compatible systems or at least to identify our data in such a way to enable its intelligent reuse. However, 'catalog it once for all' (Tillett, 1993) is not a new concept. It was a popular refrain at the beginning of the 20th century, as libraries endeavoured to share their cataloguing work. Systems like the Virtual International Authority File (VIAF) were built with the perspective of sharing the authority control activity. Data are being used for creative purposes, far beyond the original intent to identify the standard form of a name to be used in a catalogue, ready to enable any variant form of a name to access that entity.

So, as capabilities evolve, the focus of the cataloguing standards, guidelines and rules have evolved from building a bibliographic record to documenting bibliographic data, identifying the described entity to enable users to *find, identify, select* and *obtain* the information they want. These are the objectives of *Functional Requirements for Bibliographic Records* (FRBR) along with the 'navigate' function incorporated into the *International Cataloguing Principles* (ICP) and *Resource Description and Access* (RDA).

This is the fascinating realm that Professor Guerrini explores through the following publication. And who among you will now take up the challenge to move us even further to help users get the information they want?

Barbara B. Tillett, PhD

In a conversation in a faculty meeting in a leading South African LIS school in the early 1980s, I ventured the opinion that cataloguing is a central competency of any librarian. This was greeted with derision. Since then, as a manager and researcher, I have observed the practical consequences of the drift away from all library-related things towards the 'harder' and more academically respectable discipline of information science. As an ineducable dinosaur, I remain convinced of the centrality of cataloguing in the information professions. You may not have to, or want to, catalogue, but some under-standing of the principles of cataloguing is essential to almost any facet of information service. Cataloguing is not a refuge for shrinking violets or for pernickety, nit-picking, obsessive-compulsive types who become librarians because they don't like dealing with people. Cataloguing is for connecting people with resources. It is basic to the selection, acquisition/ingestion, storage, retrieval/discovery and availability of bibliographic resources of all kinds, ancient and modern, physical and virtual.

It is for this reason that I admire the work of my friend Mauro Guerrini and his Italian colleagues, who, in their teaching and research, not only give the subject the scholarly attention it deserves, but also publish guidelines and manuals for practising professionals and make the subject accessible to those of us who do not catalogue, but need to know what it involves and especially, why.

I count myself in the latter group. I was taught cataloguing in the mid-1960s, when the rules were set out in the ALA *Cataloging Rules for Author and Title Entries* of 1949, a revision of the 1908 *Cataloguing Rules*, which had been the result of a collaboration between the American Library Association and the (British) Library Association. This was a slim volume with a brick-red softcover. Roughly when I first started teaching in a library school, the 'blue code' was introduced: the *Anglo-American Cataloging Rules (AACR)* of 1967, a much thicker volume with a blue softcover. We were a small school and faculty members had to be jacks of all trades and I ended up teaching a senior cataloguing course for which I had to master this new code. That was the extent of my cataloguing experience. AACR2 and all subsequent developments largely passed me by. Not entirely, though. Some years later as the director of a national library which compiled a national bibliography and a national union catalogue, I found our cataloguers embroiled in passionate debates about MARC formats, USMARC vs. UNIMARC vs. the now forgotten South African variant, SAMARC. I learned that differences between these formats had management and financial implications for our national bibliographic functions and that turf disputes about authority control (which institution had the best cataloguers?) required diplomatic handling.

All of these issues had a significant international dimension. During the 1980s and 1990s I was involved in IFLA's Universal Bibliographic Control (UBC) and Universal Availability of Publications (UAP) programmes. Cataloguing and cataloguing standards featured prominently among the nuts and bolts of these ambitious international schemes for sharing bibliographic records and for document supply. Indeed, from my vantage point as a student and teacher of international and comparative librarianship, I appreciate that in this volume Mauro illustrates how very important both the international exchange of ideas and formal international co-operation have been in the development of contemporary cataloguing theory and principles.

Looking back at my own experience, I think that the negative reputation that cataloguing acquired among many LIS students and professionals in the past may be the result of what was taught and how. We were taught the rules. Notably absent from the syllabus in my time was the conceptual basis of cataloguing – the philosophy and principles underlying the rules. To these this book offers a concise and lucid introduction, well supplied with examples and references. Reading it filled in for me many gaps in my understanding of contemporary cataloguing and how it evolved to where we are today. It is also a very useful contribution to the study of international and comparative librarianship and information work.

Peter Lor, DPhil

Acknowledgements

The volume is a revised and updated text of the second edition of *Dalla Catalogazione alla Metadatazione: tracce di un percorso*, Roma: Associazione Italiana Biblioteche, 2022.

Barbara B. Tillett commented on the text and revised it with her competence; to Barbara my extreme gratitude for her help. Thanks to Akbari Darian for her important suggestions. Thanks to Dorothy McGarry, Peter Lor and Thomas Bourke, who kindly read and commented on the text and suggested improvements. Thanks to Pierluigi Feliciati and Lapo Ghiringhelli for their help. Denise Biagiotti and Laura Manzoni were valuable and competent interlocutors throughout the editorial process of the volume. In particular, Denise Biagiotti is the author of Section 2.3, 'Metadata: a polysemantic term'; Laura Manzoni is the author of Sections 5.2 'Relationships' and 5.5, 'Entity identifiers' and Chapter 7, 'RDA: Some Basics'.

All websites were last consulted on 30 June 2022.

List of Acronyms

AACR	Anglo-American Cataloguing Rules
AACR2	Anglo American Cataloguing Rules 2nd edition
AFSCME	American Federation of State, County and Municipal Employees
AIB	Associazione Italiana Biblioteche
ALA	American Library Association
ANNAMARC	Automazione Nella NAzionale MARC
App	Application
ARK	Archival Resource Key
BFE	BIBFRAME Editor
BIBFRAME	Bibliographic Framework
BnF	Bibliothèque nationale de France
CANMARC	Canadian MARC
CD	Compact Disc
CIDOC CRM	Comité International pour la DOCumentation – Conceptual Reference Model
DCMI	Dublin Core Metadata Initiative
DDC	Dewey Decimal Classification
DOI	Digital Object Identifier
DVD	Digital Versatile Disc
ELAG	European Library Automation Group
E-R	Entity-Relationship
FRAD	Functional Requirements for Authority Data
FRANAR	Functional Requirements and Numbering of Authority Records
FRBR	Functional Requirements for Bibliographic Records
FRBRoo	FRBR-object oriented
FR family	Functional Requirements family
FRSAD	Functional Requirements for Subject Authority Data
GLAM	Galleries, Libraries, Archives and Museums
ICCP	International Conference on Cataloguing Principles

ICCU	Istituto Centrale per il Catalogo Unico delle biblioteche e italiane e per le informazioni bibliografiche
ICP	International Cataloguing Principles
ID	Identifier
IFLA	International Federation of Library Associations and Institutions
IFLA LRM	IFLA Library Reference Model
ILS	Integrated Library System
IME ICC	IFLA Meetings of Experts on an International Cataloguing Code
INTERMARC	MARC France
IRI	Internationalised Resource Identifier
ISADN	International Standard Authority Data Number
ISBD	International Standard Bibliographic Description
ISBD(A)	ISBD for Older Monographic Publications (Antiquarian)
ISBD(An)	ISBD for Analysis
ISBD(CF)	ISBD for Computer Files
ISBD(CM)	ISBD for Cartographic Materials
ISBD(CP)	ISBD for Component Parts
ISBD(CR)	ISBD for Serials and other Continuing Resources
ISBD(ER)	ISBD for Electronic Resources
ISBD(G)	ISBD General
ISBD(M)	ISBD for Monographic Publications
ISBD(NBM)	ISBD for Non-Book Materials
ISBD(PM)	ISBD for Printed Music
ISBD(S)	ISBD for Serials
ISBN	International Standard Book Number
ISMN	International Standard Music Number
ISNI	International Standard Name Identifier
ISO	International Organisation for Standardisation
ISRC	International Standard Recording Code
ISSN	International Standard Serial Number
ISTC	International Standard Text Code
ISWC	International Standard Musical Work Code
LCSH	Library of Congress Subject Headings
LOD	Linked Open Data
MAB	Musei, Archivi e Biblioteche
MARC	MAchine Readable Cataloguing
MARCXML	MARC eXtensible Markup Language
METS	Metadata Encoding and Transmission Standard

NBN	National Bibliography Number
OCLC	Online Computer Library Center
ONIX	ONline Information eXchange
OPAC	Online Public Access Catalogue
ORCID	Open Researcher and Contributor ID
PDF	Portable Document Format
RDA	Resource Description and Access
RDA COP	RDA Committee of Principals
RDF	Resource Description Framework
REICAT	Regole italiane di catalogazione
RICA	Regole italiane di catalogazione per autori
RSC	RDA Steering Committee
SBD	Standard Bibliographic Description
SHLs	Subject Headings Languages
UAP	Universal Availability of Publications
UBC	Universal Bibliographic Control
UBICIM	Universal Bibliographic Control and International MARC Programme
UCLA	University of California, Los Angeles
UDC	Universal Decimal Classification
UKMARC	United Kingdom MARC
UNIMARC	Universal MAchine-Readable Cataloguing
URI	Uniform Resource Identifier
URL	Uniform Resource Locator
USMARC	United States MARC
VIAF	Virtual International Authority File
VIAF ID	VIAF Identifier
W3C	World Wide Web Consortium
WSDS	Web-Scale Discovery Services
WWW	World Wide Web
XML	eXtensible Markup Language

1

Cataloguing and Metadata Creation. The Centrality of a Cultural and Technical Activity

Contemporary theory has replaced the traditional cataloguing paradigm (Taylor, 1993) in favour of the adoption of metadata methodologies. The tools for the discovery of bibliographic resources[1] have been (and will increasingly be) placed within the language of the Semantic Web. This evolution accentuated the granularity and atomisation of the data. There was a breaking of the compact, closed record in favour of a new open structure. Individual data are assembled and each of them can have connections with other data through relationships. It began:

- pragmatically and on a technological level with the use of MARC in the mid-1960s
- consciously on a conceptual level with FRBR at the end of the last century.

In particular, FRBR emphasised individual elements with respect to the record as a whole. FRBR also favoured identifying the data of bibliographic resources (or simply resources) by assigning 'high', 'medium', or 'low' values to individual records.

The valuation of resources was the precondition for shifting from records management to data management, which was a process that involved identifying and connecting data related to:

- a work
- an author
- a subject.

Data are formulated through terms defined by controlled vocabularies and ontologies (the shared and explicit formal representations of specific knowledge domains).

Data management differs from traditional records management and is typical of web-based work. However, data management reinforces the rigour of bibliographic analysis (see Section 4.4) in new technological contexts. An essential argument is that the new record (or dataset) shows a higher respect for the source of information than the traditional record.

Metadata are used in every field and activity of human knowledge. They tend to describe the sets of real-world objects. Metadata may refer to or be a part of, an analogue (a person, a work, an art object, a concept, etc.) and a digital collection. Deriving from this is an extended vision of the metadata field that embraces all the *cross-domains* that are necessary for the research experience. In fact, in the Semantic Web, there is no distinction between bibliographic data and other kinds of data. There are only linked data: shareable, modular and reusable. Linked data are created, enriched and modified by organisations that are authoritatively active in their fields of specialisation. This type of digital environment has created a new way of working, and it has fostered participation and collaboration between different actors by being based on interoperable and reusable data in different domains: libraries, archives, museums, administrative, medical, legal, etc. Data or datasets can be captured and reused. They may be shaped into various forms and enriched through different procedures but maintain their identity regardless of the specific domain of use. This means that the same data can be used in a bibliographical context as well as in other seemingly disparate contexts. For example, a geographical place that is taken from the metadata of GeoNames (a service that originated in the field of geography) can be used as a link to cite a source's place of publication.

The sharing of data for the purposes of interoperability, the reuse of data in different domains and the ability of a datum to interact with other existing or still developing data (without any access restrictions) are important capabilities. The web, particularly the Semantic Web, is essentially democratic. It makes the exchange of data possible. One example is the publication and reuse of data with Linked Open Data (LOD) technology addressed to users and software agents. The shift from the textual record to data is marked by the introduction of the Linked Open Data paradigm, which has generated a major shift in perspective and continues to redefine the concept of cataloguing.

Metadata creation, in the field of library science, refers to the dimension of cataloguing in the digital age. It is the process of recording metadata, which are data that are essential to the identification and retrieval of a resource. Metadata, literally data about data, are structured information about other data. In other words, they are sets of information describing other information. They derive from the resource itself and sometimes from bibliographic directories. Metadata facilitate interoperability, a term that refers to the search, retrieval, management, and reuse of data.

Put simply, metadata creation is the creation of metadata for a co-ordinated and structured information system. The process, through which one moves from data to metadata, involves the identification of:

- the application context (e.g. bibliographic, administrative, medical, legal)
- the significant types of information (e.g. for a book: title, author, edition, place and date of publication)
- the subsequent 'capture' and management of the information, its reprocessing and application for specific needs.

Perspective and logic are changed and transformed into metadata creation. Metadata creation maintains and strengthens the distinctive characteristic of being, first and foremost, a cultural activity that implies the knowledge of the resource (what it is, of whom it is). It is therefore, a technical activity (which implies the knowledge of professional languages). Ultimately, the modalities of the procedures to be performed have changed once again. Consider how often they have changed from Callimachus' time to today (Callimachus was a 3rd-century Greek scholar, librarian and cataloguer at the Library of Alexandria, who created *Pinakes*, a comprehensive bibliography of all Greek literature at the time). Nevertheless, there is no change in the deeper meaning of cataloguing as a procedure of conscious mediation between the collection (and each individual resource) and the reader. A dogmatic spirit cannot characterise the philosophy of the educational approach to cataloguing. Rather, it requires critical thinking and a recognition of the editorial and historical complexity of the bibliographic object to be described.

The catalogue of the present and the future (whether it continues to be called this or by another name), will consequently continue to play a central role in the web. Since the web itself is characterised by the absence of a centre, the catalogue cannot be at the centre of the web. Instead, the catalogue functions as a tool that reflects the collaborative capacity of libraries to build a controlled process and to offer quality data (Oddy, 1996).

In this context the relevance of cataloguing is reinvigorated, supported by a 'great tradition' that Gorman effectively outlined in Seymour Lubetzky's *laudatio* on the occasion of his 100th birthday celebration held at the University of California, Los Angeles (UCLA) on 18 April 1998. He expanded on the parallelism made by the literary critic F. R. Leavis, when he traced the grand tradition of the English novel to George Eliot, ending with D. H. Lawrence (Leavis, 1948).

English-language descriptive cataloguing has its own *Great tradition* that began
with Antonio Panizzi's *91 Rules* and reached its most recent peak in the work of
Seymour Lubetzky. Because of his influence and the power of his ideas, it can
truly be said that the most suitable title for a history of Anglo-American
cataloguing would be 'From Panizzi to Lubetzky'.

(Gorman, 2000)

Cataloguing is a tradition that begins with Panizzi's *Rules* in 1841, and
continues with *On the Construction of Catalogs of Libraries*, published by
the Smithsonian Institution in 1852 and the definitive edition in 1853,
written by Charles Coffin Jewett (Jewett, 1853). The tradition then develops
and consolidates with Charles Ammi Cutter between the 19th and 20th
centuries, culminating with Lubetzky's two most important works: *Code of
Cataloging Rules: author and title entry* (Lubetzky, 1960) and *Principles of
Cataloging* (Lubetzky, 1969).

'The changes in cataloguing techniques, linked to the transformation and
multiplication of supports' – as interpreted by the Italian librarian Carlo
Revelli – 'do not negate the foundations of the traditional line drawn by
Cutter, since the legendary year 1876' (Revelli, 2014). Therefore, there is
an evolution in cataloguing, whose methodology consists of acts of
interpretation and evaluation. Cataloguing is not the simple application of
norms; it is an activity that requires competence, time, energy, skills and
responsibility (Cerbo, 2011).

2

Panta Rei

Nothing ever stays the same, or, as Heraclitus
put it, *panta rei* – everything flows.

2.1 Metanoia

For at least two decades, cataloguing has been experiencing a second cultural and technological revolution after that of the 1970s. It is characterised by the transition from the paper paradigm to the automation paradigm. Understanding what cataloguing means today, in the digital environment, requires those who are starting to learn it to have an attitude of great attention: its procedures are complex and are being redesigned. For those already familiar with cataloguing, the new digital context requires a further paradigm shift: it requires metanoia, 'a change of mind', an open intellectual disposition; a conscious disposition and one not conditioned by conventions, which are always provisional.

Rethinking the cataloguing tradition serves:

- to understand which procedures are worth continuing and developing and
- which procedures were innovative in their time but exhausted their 'driving force'.

The web has changed the reader's behaviour and has therefore affected the user functions, the ways of *finding, identifying, selecting* and *obtaining* information and resources, the ways of exploring the bibliographic universe. The web is the place where most searches take place. Many readers have perceived the distance between the bibliographic universe surveyed by the catalogues and the enormous amount of information available online and accessible through search engines. Therefore, users start – and often conclude – their research without consulting catalogues (Dunsire and Willer, 2013).

We can identify four macro contexts in which the web has made a significant change:

1 *technological context*: the advent of the web, in particular the Semantic Web, offers different tools, with new possibilities for formalising and using data
2 *social context*: the users prefer using search engines as the main tools in finding information for their bibliographic researches. They demand to be able to move and interact with the catalogues with the same autonomy and independence used on the web
3 *information context*: the proliferation of new types of digital resources that the traditional catalogue is no longer able to manage
4 *general cultural context*: many users have lost the sense of the qualitative hierarchy of sources and that of the provenance of cultural information, of any kind. In everyday contexts, there is a tendency not to verify whether a source is authoritative and if its provenance is reliable. This is true in every field (health, law, politics, professions, etc.) and moreover, the need for bibliographic reliability is diminished or eliminated.

From the bibliographic records management through a database, we pass (and sometimes have passed) to the direct management of data, as in other areas. *The centrality of data has substituted for the centrality of the record*. The drafting of structured records in pre-established areas marked by conventional punctuation, as required by ISBD, has been replaced by a process of *identification* and *linking* of data.

Each technical change involves changes in procedures and results. The transition from book catalogues to card catalogues enabled a faster and less expensive updating of the catalogue. The subsequent move to the electronic catalogue imposed coding and authority files management and has overcome the limitations of single physical sorting sequences. This made it possible to offer opportunities for different sorting and grouping. In particular, the electronic catalogue has extended the search from headings to the text of descriptions. Today, the transition to the web catalogue dismembers the record data package and links the identification of the represented entities and their independent registration. This new dimension makes data available for any application beyond the occasional source outside the context of the library.

The difference between the two processes is well explained, briefly, by Carlo Bianchini:

> The material product resulting from the two processes of cataloguing and metadata creation is different. Cataloguing produces a catalogue, that is a list of records relating to various types of resources, ordered and searchable according

to a defined criterion, on the basis of which the catalogue was constructed: by author, by title, by class, by subject, etc. Metadata creation, on the other hand, produces the metadata of the resources, but the methods of access to the descriptions and the structure of presentation of data are open and they can be defined *a posteriori*. Thanks to metadata, it is possible to obtain the same arrangements and the same structured presentation of information as in the printed card or in electronic catalogue displays, but also much, much more.

(Bianchini, 2022, 109–10).

With the metadata paradigm, data can be assembled and visualised in multiple ways. It is no longer necessary for the selected dataset to coincide with its presentation, that is, with its visualisation. Data are free to be aggregated in different ways, provided, of course, that it is always done logically and not arbitrarily. The deconstruction of the record generates a remarkable transformation on a conceptual level, with obvious repercussions on the mediation tools between the bibliographic universe and the reader. For example, 'monolithic' registration:

```
Our enduring values, revisited : librarianship in an ever-changing
world / Michael Gorman. — Chicago : American Library
Association, 2015. — 240 p. — ISBN 978-0-8389-1300-0.
```

can be broken down into its individual constituent data:

- Our enduring values, revisited – title proper
- librarianship in an ever-changing world – other title information
- Michael Gorman – statement of responsibility relating to the title proper
- Chicago – place of publication
- American Library Association – publisher's name
- 2015 – date of publication
- 240 p. – extent
- ISBN 978-0-8389-1300-0 – identifier for manifestation (see Section 2.2)

User behaviours have been greatly influenced, over the last few years, by three further technological transformations:

1 the pervasiveness of networks using wireless connections (Wi-Fi) ensures continuous and ubiquitous connectivity
2 the diffusion of personal mobile devices (tablets, smartphones, etc.), voice recognition techniques, specialised apps capable of receiving updated data sent from sources of information using PUSH technology[2]

3 the increasing adoption of artificial intelligence (AI) algorithms that assist and guide users in carrying out activities and functions.

The combined effect of these disruptive innovations has led to a significant and irreversible transformation of human–machine interaction methods, which even libraries cannot ignore (Spitzer, 2012).

Hence a recurring question: have the spread of the web, the current technologies and the enormous availability of online content made the role of catalogues and, in general, of libraries themselves marginal? If not obsolete? The answer is: certainly not. Not even an initiative like Google Books has superseded them. However, it is undeniable that the new cultural and technological context has prompted libraries to rethink deeply the composition, availability and use of their collections, unifying the services linked to analogue and digital collections. Libraries have always played and continue to play a crucial role in the conservation, protection, enhancement and use of recorded knowledge. The problem of disintermediation (doing without research tools and even those who create them) exists but is under control. Tools such as web-scale discovery services (WSDS) place the user in a condition of apparent disintermediation.

In this changed situation, cataloguing is not abandoned. If anything, it is enriched, but inevitably it has to adapt to the new context, as Alan Danskin argues authoritatively in the report presented at the IFLA Congress in Seoul, Korea, in 2006:

> First of all, what does 'cataloguing' mean? For the purposes of this paper, I have adopted a broad definition incorporating the following activities:
>
> • Description of the resource sufficient for purposes of identification and for differentiation from other similar resources
> • Identification and control of access points
> • Identification and control of relationships with other resources
> • Subject analysis of the resource
> • Assignment of subject indexing terms
> • Assignment of classification numbers.
>
> The challenges facing cataloguing are all too well known. In no particular order, the major challenges are:
>
> • Increasing inputs
> • New kinds of information resources
> • Competition from other mediation services

- Perception that cataloguing is high cost and offers poor value for money
- Fiscal constraints
- Declining workforce.

This is a daunting list.

(Danskin, 2006 205–9)

What can we do? The British librarian asks himself:

From this review of the challenges, two key questions arise:

1 Is cataloguing still relevant in the web environment and will it remain relevant in the medium to long term?
2 If cataloguing is still relevant, how does it need to change to meet these challenges?

In the short to medium term, the answer must be a resounding 'yes'.

(Danskin, 2006, 205).

The relationships between the library and readers have changed. Cataloguers have accepted the challenge posed by the web and contemporary technologies. They have adopted the typical language of the digital era and, have proposed a new philosophy, the result of a long reflection carried out mainly in the IFLA context and at the most representative levels of the library profession (International Conference on the Principles and Future Development of AACR, 1998; Conference on Bibliographic Control for the New Millennium, 2001).

2.2 New concepts and new terminology

In a phase of new theoretical formulations for cataloguing and the starting of a delicate, difficult and non-linear transition towards new types of catalogues, the bibliographic models of the *Functional Requirements* (FR) family – *Functional Requirements for Bibliographic Records* (FRBR), *Functional Requirements for Authority Data* (FRAD) and *Functional Requirements for Subject Authority Data* (FRSAD), and now the IFLA *Library Reference Model* (IFLA LRM) – all issued by IFLA – have represented and still represent a basic reference both for their content and for the terminology used or introduced (Pisanski and Žumer, 2010). Consequently, it is necessary first to define the meaning of some concepts and terms.

The *bibliographic universe* is a formulation that entered the language of librarianship at the end of the 20th century. The term was codified by FRBR

(Tillett, 2008) and can be defined as the set of knowledge recorded on any medium transmitted over time by the human community and accessible in libraries, archives, museums and on the web.

The bibliographic universe includes any type of resource in its analogue and digital dimension and the persons and the institutions responsible for them or those who play any role in them. The appearance of new varieties of resources typical of the digital world and of new ways of reading texts, watching images and listening to music produces constant changes. The publishing technologies designed in recent decades open the possibility of enjoying the same work in multiple versions, formats or presentations: as a printed volume, audiobook, e-book (in pdf, html, epub, mobi) or digital book. The last of these is a book form that we could define as two-dimensional. It consists of content and metadata that are inextricably associated like two sides of the same coin. The relationship established between the content of a work and its metadata recalls the image of an iceberg: the content consists of the emerging part of the ice block, while the metadata are represented by the submerged part that allows the emerging part to float (Guatelli, 2020).

The bibliographic universe has deeply changed with the presence, gradually increasing since the end of the last century, of intangible digital resources. This has inaugurated a brand-new paradigm both in the organisation and use of data and resources and in the research methods used to create them. Virtual collections have been born and have been described with increasingly precise and sophisticated definition, often in a free mode (open access), of texts, sounds and images. All this has opened up the possibility of previously unthinkable investigations.

The innovations in the bibliographic universe have had consequences at a terminological level. Some phrases have acquired a different meaning (as happens in every living language) and neologisms have been coined. We use fewer and fewer terms such as *document, cataloguing, catalogue, record* and more and more words such as *agent, creator, data, dataset, discovery, element, entity, format, instance, item, metadata, resource, tag, triple,* derived almost all from the IT field or the Semantic Web context. The term *cataloguing* continues to be used in many realities with a wider meaning than in the past. New job titles have appeared, such as *metadata manager, data manager, data curation librarian, data reference librarian, data collection building librarian.*

Entities, in the new metadata perspective, are *identified* and *connected,* as explained in FRBR, IFLA LRM and BIBFRAME – which we will talk about later – through relationships. The network of relationships allows the reader to navigate between entities and find the resources they need more easily than in the past.

Document, a term widely used since the second half of the 20th century, is now excluded in the *International Cataloguing Principles* (ICP) published by IFLA in 2009; its use is restricted to the archival context and replaced by *bibliographic resource* or *resource*.

The term *resource* denotes an entity, analogue or digital, including an intellectual or artistic content (or both), conceived, produced and published as a separate unit. It refers to all possible forms and all possible vehicles of knowledge, that is, to all types of material preserved in libraries and other cultural institutions of recorded memory: manuscripts, ancient and modern books, e-books, serials, sheet music and music performances, fixed and moving images (a video disc, a video game, a film), geographical maps, photographs, sound recordings, archival documents, art objects and found objects of all kinds in an analogue or digital dimension. *Resource* represents, in short, an all-encompassing formulation of everything that is part of a traditional library or a digital library. It includes individual entities or could aggregate components of such entities (e.g. three sheets of geographical maps, the paper contained in an issue of a journal). It may indicate a tangible entity (e.g. a paper book) or an intangible entity (e.g. a website). *The British Library's Collection Metadata Strategy*, in its Glossary, offers this definition: 'Structured information that describes, explains, locates or otherwise makes it easier to retrieve, use or manage an information resource'.[3]

Carlo Bianchini, reflecting on the ongoing terminological changes, states:

The new terminology is intended to highlight the change that has taken place in the approach to the representation and exploitation of the collections of cultural institutions. Museum and library catalogues and archive inventories used to be tools to find the items stored in collections. With the advent of the Semantic Web, it must be recognised that the information contained in these tools can perform not only that task, but many others and that it is a resource with enormous cultural, social and even economic asset. For this reason, metadata have shifted the focus from just information about cultural heritage (for example, a book, a document, a work of art) to all the multiple information that can be retrieved about any entity represented by the metadata contained in the retrieval tools. In this perspective, all data provided on collections are a resource, not only those related to a particular item, for example, a particular event or a specific copy of it (bibliographic resource). Any data about a work or an expression of it, a person, a place (such as a city, an administrative subdivision, an environment) or a time span (such as a day, a year or an era) and regardless of whether that data was created by a library, a museum, an archive or any other authoritative agency is a common, public, and shareable resource. The term resource in the context of the Semantic Web denotes all these entities and their data; it implies a broader and more inclusive view of the data function of a retrieval tool and it is useful and usable because it is transversal, that is, it allows crossing the boundary of a specific cultural institution. This is very important because the approach of the citizen searching for information about a person or a work, for instance, is (has always been) all-round and the information he or she receives in response should no longer be limited to the information a specific institution – library, archive or museum – owns or makes accessible. Resource is a term that allows for proper interaction with all the other actors contributing to the growth of the Semantic Web; in order to have a dialogue, a common language is needed.

(Bianchini, 2022, 131).

According to the entity identification process proposed by FRBR and then by IFLA LRM, we have:

- *Item*: the unit; in case of a book, it is the single witness, the single copy of a set of identical copies
- *Manifestation:* a set of all carriers that are assumed to share the same characteristics as to intellectual or artistic content and aspects of physical form. That set is defined by both the overall content and the production plan for its carrier or carriers (IFLA LRM, 2017, 25)
- *Expression*: the intellectual and artistic realisation of a work
- *Work*: a specific artistic or intellectual creation.

Aggregates are a type of resource in which multiple expressions of single or multiple works are included in a manifestation. Typical examples are:

- anthologies and lessons, in which various texts are published in a *manifestation* for which the intellectual contribution of the curator is recognised
- a text with a parallel translation, with two expressions of the same work (original text and translated text)
- resources where a main and independent work is supplemented by additional text, such as an introduction, a comment, accompanying illustrations, e.g. *Robinson Crusoe* by Daniel Defoe, with an introduction for teachers by Edward R. Shaw.

The IFLA LRM glossary (IFLA LRM, 2017, 100) defines the concepts of *Entity, Attribute, Instance, Relationship* as:

- *Entity*: 'An abstract class of conceptual objects, representing the key objects of interest in the model' (IFLA LRM, 2017, 100). They are: Work, Expression, Manifestation, Item, Person, Corporate Body, etc.
- *Attribute*: 'A type of data which characterises specific instances of an entity' (IFLA LRM, 2017, 100) (e.g. extent of a manifestation, the profession of a person)
- *Instance*: 'A specific exemplar of an entity' (IFLA LRM, 2017, 100) (e.g. the edition *Don Quixote* by Cervantes in the Italian series I Meridiani, as an instance of the entity *manifestation*; Florence as an instance of the entity *place*)
- *Relationship*: 'A connection between instances of entities' (IFLA LRM, 2017, 100) (e.g. between the instance of the entity work *Robinson Crusoe* and the instance of entity person *Daniel Defoe* or between the instance of the entity work *Robinson Crusoe* and the instance of the entity corporate body *University Publishing Company* that published the novel in New York–Boston in 1897).

ICP explicitly excludes the use of terms such as *Bibliographic Unit* in favour of *Manifestation*; *Heading* in favour of *Authorized access point* or *Controlled access point*; *Reference* in favour of *Variant form of name*; *Uniform title* in favour of *Authorized access point, Authorized form of name* or *Name*.

The passage from the title *Functional Requirements for Bibliographic Records* to *Functional Requirements for Authority Data* is emblematic. The terminological change (from *record* in the title of FRBR to *data* in the title of FRAD) denotes the conceptual shift that took place between the 20th and 21st centuries. It is worth noting that the semi-final version of ICP of December 2008 had proposed the term *record* in the text but the final report – presented at the IFLA Congress of Milan, Italy, on 24 August 2009 – shows *data*. This conceptual shift is also reflected in the list of terms no longer in use in ICP2016: *Authority record* is replaced by *Authority data*, *Bibliographic record* is replaced by *Bibliographic data*.

Navigate is a term reflecting a typical concept of the digital era. It refers to moving across a connection between entities. It assumes a network of relationships between works, editions (expressions, manifestations) and authors, contributors, publishers and other actors of the book supply chain. The relationships place each entity in connection with others, creating networks that can become very rich: relationships between the entity work and agent (person or corporate body) with the role of creator, contributor (author of a foreword, translator . . .), publisher, subject, etc. Relationships allow the reader to discover the desired resources and to find other semantically and functionally similar resources.

The function of navigating between entities, between data different by type and origin, was launched by Elaine Svenonius.[4] This function is foreshadowed in FRBR (paragraph 5.1 and then taken up by ICP), whose initial drafting was done by Svenonius together with Tom Delsey and Barbara B. Tillett.[5] Svenonius talks about navigation in her fundamental work for contemporary cataloguing theory *The Intellectual Foundation of Information Organization* (Svenonius, 2000), where she summarises the topics of cataloguing within a common conceptual framework.[6] Navigation is the experience of finding what you are looking for and something not already known. This has always happened with any type of catalogue: travelling on bibliographic paths that were not initially foreseen, following increasingly complex and unexpected paths. In contrast, we use the term *serendipity*, meaning the free, unexpected and surprising discovery of something interesting for the ongoing investigations.[7]

2.3 Metadata: a polysemantic term

A *datum* (from the Latin *datum*, meaning 'gift, given thing') is a codified elementary description of a piece of information, an entity of a phenomenon, transaction and event. ISO 5127:2017 presents only the plural *data*, defined as a 'reinterpretable representation of information in a formalized manner suitable for communication, interpretation or processing' (ISO 5127).

Data are represented in many forms: text, images, video, sound and many others. We speak of statistical and mathematical data or of databases. By extension, we speak of personal data, with reference to everything that concerns the private or public life of a person. For administrative functions, we require data to fill in forms or fulfil multiple needs. Data are susceptible to processing, storage and dissemination. They may be stored on different media – physical such as paper, magnetic, optical, digital (CDs, DVDs, hard disks, etc.) – or they may be transmitted via a telecommunications network between several users (e.g. Wikipedia).

The birth of a metadata system is linked to a need for research, unambiguous identification, synthesis and management of a dataset. For instance, metadata allow a book to be located in a library catalogue and on Amazon or any digital platform for purchase; a piece of music to be found on YouTube; a person to be located on Facebook or Instagram. Metadata are born to solve a problem or to perform a function.

'Metadata' is a relatively new word. It appeared in the second half of the 20th century, but came into common use in librarianship when we moved from implicit metadata management to its logical formalisation. Formalisation implies the availability of a conceptual model for managing bibliographic data.

Metadata are sets of information describing other information. The ISO 5127:2017 standard defines them as 'data about other data, documents or records that describes their content, context, structure, provenance and/or rights attached to them' (ISO 5127:2017).

The term metadata consists of the Greek prefix μ (*meta*: 'beyond, after, above') and *data*, the Latin neuter plural of *datum*. The prefix 'meta-' is often used to describe a new discipline designed to address the original one critically. It denotes a change, a transformation, a permutation or a substitution. It is used in this sense in the term 'metaphysics'. It has since been extended to numerous other disciplines. The origin of the term in contemporary times can be traced back to the IT environment, in particular the context of databases. It takes on different meanings in relation to different domains and functions and this makes it difficult to present an unambiguous definition of the concept.

The concept itself exists in many information contexts. When we look at a digital image on the web, its properties, such as, for instance, size, date, format, are its related metadata. The same applies to a Word document or any file whose attributes are known. Metadata are a kind of 'qualifier' of the resource that allow its correct characterisation. They are the necessary and sufficient characteristics to identify a resource and link it to other relevant resources. Metadata qualify every single attribute of an entity: bibliographic (such as work, title, author, contributor, publisher) or otherwise. The term has been adopted to describe datasets within the various scientific communities, for example for the data records of a research project or a patient's medical data. It has been used since 1994 by the geophysical community for geospatial data: names, availability, relevance to given uses, access method, transfer mode (Dillon, 2000).

The etymology of the word and the almost tautological definition – *data on data* – accentuate the link between *data*, that is, the main information of a resource, and *metadata*, the information related to the resource itself. Metadata are essential to describe the resource, locate it and retrieve it. Metadata, in other words, are that set of information that uniquely identifies a resource in any context.

Cataloguing is an action of data production, with reference to a given object, digital or physical. In the exercise of their activity, the cataloguers do nothing more than report information, data, structured according to a defined modality, that represent certain aspects of, say, a book, with the aim to support user research. The *data* are initially transformed into *metadata* and then *metadata* become *data* again. So, it is evident how cataloguing is configured as an action of creating metadata, in its strictest sense as the creation of structured data (Long, 2016).

There remains, therefore, the question of how cataloguing differs from metadata creation, the origin of which should be interpreted as an extension, typical of the digital age. The use of the term metadata must, in fact, be appropriately contextualised within the crossing of boundaries that has affected both the collection and the library's tools. The gradual transition from second-generation OPACs towards what are defined as *web-scale discovery tools* has implied the passage from a tool substantially focused on the management and presentation of the library's physical collection to a unitary system of access to data from a variety of sources, whether they derive from specialised domain databases, commercial suppliers or bibliographic citation databases. The use of the term metadata reveals a willingness to open up to a more multifaceted reality, a way of addressing other modes and interlocutors that rely on different but no less rigorous rules and methodologies of data creation.

Therefore, logically, cataloguing and metadata creation are not radically different. It depends on the context of reference, since it is, substantially, the application of the same activity, that is data creation: creation of more strictly catalographic data for printed resources,[8] creation of data in the broadest sense of any type and in any application context, even outside libraries.

2.4 Libraries, Semantic Web and linked data: the data librarian

The conceptual and terminological change has consequences on the management side. The offices of many large libraries are no longer named Cataloguing Department, but, for example, at the Bibliothèque nationale de France (BnF), this office is called *Département des métadonnées*; at the British Library initially *Collection and Metadata Processing* and now simply *Metadata*; at the Stanford University Libraries *Metadata Department* and at numerous American and Canadian libraries *Metadata Services*. Many cataloguers, especially Americans, prefer to call themselves 'metadata creation manager', as at the Harvard Library Information and Technical Services Department. In contrast, a *Metatada editor* is the name of the tool with which bibliographic, authority and holding metadata are displayed and edited in Alma, the Harvard bibliographic system.

Since 2015, the three IFLA sections Bibliography, Cataloguing and Subject Analysis and Access have started to publish the 'IFLA Metadata Newsletter'. At the Bodleian Library in Oxford, England, an *Ask a data librarian* service has been opened within the Bodleian Data Library, with the presence of a *data librarian*.

The 'data librarian' is increasingly emerging as a multi-faceted and dynamic professional figure. The term takes on different connotations, depending on the stage of the data life cycle and the different application contexts.

The data librarians are information professionals who possess the cultural and technical skills to manage data (*data management*). They are librarians who use data as a resource and who are able to educate users on the conscious use of such data, because they have a holistic view of library science methods and principles, comparable to other professionals working in data science.

Similar terminology change has affected the traditional concept of *information literacy*, which is evolving into that of *data literacy* (Si et al., 2013). Data literacy includes all the activities of supporting the user throughout the process of data management. Information reaches the user with a minimum of context (the book, the journal, the web page), while data are often unstructured. This is why applying data literacy is fundamental. Users, overwhelmed by data, need to understand them, contextualise them, identify their limits and potential. This is one of the main tasks of a data librarian, as illustrated in Figure 2.1.

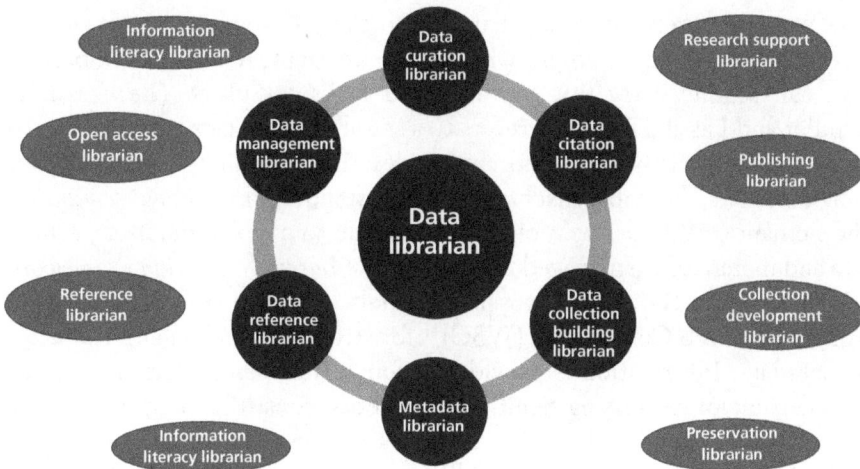

Figure 2.1 *The activities of a data librarian*

In *Our Enduring Values, Revisited* (Gorman, 2015), published by the American Library Association (ALA), Michael Gorman, who played a notable role in the contemporary American and international library community, defines cataloguing and classification as the most intellectual sphere of librarianship. Of course, each library service requires both intellectual and managerial strength, as the construction of a collection shows. Theories often arise from the recognition of a state of crisis, when a choice is required to face new situations and contexts, such as the emergence of new types of resources or the awareness of the ineffectiveness of the standards and codes adopted up to then. This is a phenomenon that happened in the past and is still happening today.

The invention of the world wide web (WWW), or simply the web, is an 'event' that has radically changed how we relate to information and available resources. It is the place where we express a large part of our professional and private selves. Along with the web, the appearance of search engines has transformed how to discover and access available data. For example, many applications have abandoned the presentation of search results in alphabetical order in favour of the order of *relevance*.[9]

The internet has also stimulated a greater collaboration between publishers and libraries and, at least in intention, between the institutions of recorded memory: libraries, archives and museums. Collaborative initiatives have arisen under the acronym GLAM: Galleries, Libraries, Archives and Museums.

The *Semantic Web* is a term introduced by Tim Berners-Lee. As he stated, 'The Semantic Web will bring structure to the meaningful content of web pages, creating an environment where software agents roaming from page to page can readily carry out sophisticated tasks for users' (Berners-Lee, Hendler and Lassila, 2001). It refers to a set of technologies based on *linked data* and standards where resources are described and linked to each other using metadata, to enable machines to understand their meaning: *semantics*. The Semantic Web is a web of data, traceable to a global database, where data and metadata are managed through the *Resource Description Framework* (RDF),[10] one of the various possible models proposed since 1997 by the World Wide Web Consortium (W3C)[11] for structured coding and exchange of metadata. Information is provided through *statements*, that is, minimal units capable of expressing significant concepts, consisting of an *RDF triple* (subject-object-predicate). RDF provides a shared language, capable of mediating and communicating the different data models used and allowing interoperability between applications sharing and reusing data on the web.

The transition from the web of documents (publication of texts with structured data) to the web of data (publication of texts also with structured data for reuse and retrieval by computers) has a radical impact: a greater granularity of data. Logical structure and granularity (or atomisation) are decisive concepts in the theoretical elaboration that led to the overcoming of the traditional cataloguing paradigm in favour of the adoption of metadata methodologies and coding standards that characterise the Semantic Web (Malmsten, 2012; McCallum, 2016; Guerrini and Possemato, 2015).

Over the last two decades, the initial web of documents has evolved into the web of data, in which relationships, that is qualified links, are established between data and no longer between documents. The semantic enrichment of the data, obtained by adding further meaning to the original data, makes it possible to generate value networks in which metadata constitute the various nodes. In the web of documents, information is sought not for its meaning but as strings, whereas in the Semantic Web computers are able to retrieve, interpret and reuse collections of structured data, using inference rules to support automatic reasoning.

Linked data represent a method of exposing, sharing and connecting data via their address, expressed with a *Uniform Resource Identifier* (URI). A distinctive feature is linking data with other data sets. They constitute the ideal key to build a global web (Coyle, 2013). A URI is applicable to any object and any object with a URI can be identified and processed on the web. The *Uniform Resource Locator* (URL), one of the most common types of URIs, is an address that allows visiting a web page, indicating to the client computer where to find a resource (Schreur, 2020). The identified data become autonomous, self-consistent, usable and reusable in different contexts and representations.

Linked open data (LOD) are data created using the linked data technology. In addition to being manipulated, linkable and indexable by search engines, they are *open* and freely accessible. *Ontologies* are shared and explicit formal representations of specific knowledge domains. They play an essential role in making LOD possible. Ontologies allow the representation of entities by describing their characteristics and identifying their existing relationships. They are helpful for search functions, because they enable the narrowing or expanding of a field of investigation by browsing the interconnectedness of linked concepts (Dunsire, 2012b).

2.5 Metadata and bibliographic control

Cataloguing, in the contemporary age, is part of *Universal Bibliographic Control* (UBC), an important initiative promoted by IFLA and other organisations since the Seventies to promote the sharing of bibliographic data by eliminating redundancies and encouraging the reuse of such data. The initiative foresees that each national bibliographic agency catalogues the resources published in its own country (in some cases even those published elsewhere but thematically related to its own country) and establishes the structure and form of the preferred name for the person, the corporate body and/or the work chosen for access to bibliographic records. The data products thus become shareable and reusable easily by other agencies and libraries around the world.

Giovanni Solimine, in his work *Universal Bibliographic Control* of 1995 comments:

> The bibliographic control programme intends to resume and realise in current terms and according to the canons of modern librarianship an ancient aspiration of the community of scholars and librarians and bibliographers to dominate the universe of knowledge recorded in book production, which, in different historical periods, has given rise to various attempts to compile general universal bibliographies.
>
> (Solimine, 1995, 5)

These attempts started with Conrad Gesner's *Bibliotheca Universalis*.[12]

Gordon Dunsire took up the concept of *Bibliotheca Universalis* when he defined the bibliographic universe. It is the set of all the products of human speech (that is, of all bibliographic resources) that make up the collective memory of Homo Sapiens. Bibliographic control, in turn, is defined as the cataloguing management of the bibliographic universe aimed at the access and use of resources. Dunsire argues that the bibliographic universe needs to be controlled because the legacy of recorded memory is essential to cultural identity and the bibliographic universe constitutes its heritage. The future of bibliographic control is as unpredictable as the future of the historical innovations of writing, printing, telecommunication or the internet. Dunsire views these four innovations as having had such an impact on recorded memory that they have led to its division into different *Information Ages*.

According to Dunsire, the First Information Age is the pre-literate period before the invention of writing; the Second one begins with that fundamental invention. The Third Information Age starts with the mechanisation of printing, while the Fourth one begins with the invention of telecommunication. The present is the Fifth Information Age, and it begins with the invention of the internet.

The development of metadata for bibliographic control originated in what Dunsire defines as the Third Information Age, in which, with the mechanisation of printing, modern libraries developed. We can consider metadata printing as a consequence of book printing. Dunsire continues by observing that current approaches to metadata are linked to the paradigms of the Third and Fourth Ages, the latter linked to the invention of digital communication. In the current Fifth Information Age, recorded discourse is the cultural memory and metadata creation is the organisation of culture itself.

Bibliographic control has the aim and function of managing cultural identity in a global framework. The distinction between data and metadata is no longer useful and bibliographic control becomes indistinguishable from culture itself (Dunsire, 2021).

2.6 The importance of the catalogue

The catalogue has always been and remains the heart of library services. In the second half of the 19th century, the German librarian, philologist and professor of librarianship Karl Dziatzko affirmed that the catalogue is the soul (*die Seele*) of a library (Dziatzko, 1886). Without a catalogue the library would be an indistinct and irrecoverable set of resources. All of its services hinge on it, namely reference, circulation/lending capabilities, including local and interlibrary loan, acquisitions, as the catalogue allows verification of what is owned and the rejection of what is considered obsolete or no longer to be part of the collection.

Shiyali Ramamrita Ranganathan introduces the catalogue with these words:

> The library catalogue presents a bundle of conventions. It is even treacherous.
> For, it appears to be in a familiar, natural language. But, in reality, the language of the catalogue is an artificial one. The treachery is due to its using ordinary words. Its words are not morphologically or radically artificial. But its syntax is artificial. Its semantics too is artificial. The use of punctuation marks is not all orthodox. The words in a name-of-person are inverted. All these puzzle a freshman.
>
> (Ranganathan, 1961, 89).

The catalogue, today as in the past, is the main tool of mediation between the collections of any library and users. However, library policies govern what of a library's collection is actually included in the catalogue. Some catalogues include all available resources, including direct access to digital resources available in PDF (or other formats) or online (via a link). Some other catalogues do not report links to digitally owned magazines, photos or videos; and some others do not catalogue books or databases, deferring their discovery to other discovery tools.

A collection of resources, even when selected with specific criteria, does not constitute a library in the absence of a *language* and a tool that connects it with readers. The language and tool are the *catalogue*. Its purpose is to communicate the metadata that identify what is owned by a library (or by a library system) and to enable access. Language is architecture: the catalogue reflects the depth of definition of purposes and objectives for the library and for its users.

The etymology derives from the late Latin word *catalogus* (which has its roots in the Greek term κατάλογος (*katalogos*, 'list'). Historically, the catalogue has been an instrument governed, albeit with different complexities, under constant, coherent and transparent criteria that have guaranteed its appropriate use in its specific contexts. To be effective, the catalogue is modelled on the concrete needs of each library. It is functional to its public and it addresses and shuns any abstractness or ambiguity.

The catalogue is based on a technical language and, like any language, takes into account the local practices of citing resources, social habits of its intended users, cultural and editorial conventions used in its country and technological developments. The catalogue also may take into account and even interact with other communication tools (directories, websites of publishing houses, authority file databases, etc.). From these tools, the catalogue draws the data and, at the same time, enters the data.

The quality of the data contained in a catalogue reflects the degree of knowledge that the cataloguers have of the library's collections (the level of analysis and description, of connection to other sources, etc.), of the standards of networks and co-operative projects in which the library participates and of the needs of the library's users. The catalogue assumes a common language with its readers. Some specific aspects of this language – *stability* and *coherence*, on the one hand, *expandability* and *adequacy* on the other – allow the reader to raise his or her level of success in using the catalogue.

> The ability to go beyond the daily activity and the specifics of the profession, the curiosity towards the world must characterise the future of the cataloguing profession, since the catalogues are not [...] detached from the context, but they must be inserted into the cultural and communicative flow of society in order to be and continue to be effective and efficient tools for communication, recovery and knowledge creation.
>
> (Sardo, 2017, 229)

This will inevitably be the salient feature of the catalogue in the near future. Indeed, it will continue to reflect and disseminate knowledge production processes and be an authoritative source for the reader. It is precisely this authority, due to the librarians' professional work, that perpetuates the most essential value of the catalogue and the library. As Tiziana Possemato states:

> The world of cultural heritage has a very long tradition in the history of creating and sharing structured metadata. For libraries, catalogues have always represented a set of metadata, starting with book catalogues, passing through printed cards, local terminals up to web publication and the current reformulation in terms of linked data: the attention and forces of theorists and cataloguers have always focused on increasingly structured and shareable forms

of metadata. Cataloguing means, therefore, creating metadata: it means identifying, selecting, structuring data (attributes) on data (title, author, etc.) in order to represent a resource, expressing its physical, conceptual and relationship characteristics in such a way as to make it identifiable and, therefore, usable, to those who seek it.

(Possemato, 2022, 121)

2.7 Two pitfalls for cataloguing and the catalogue?

In recent decades, two different phenomena have been seen as pitfalls of cataloguing: outsourcing and automation.

In 2004 in the article 'La Mattanza dei Catalogatori' ('The slaughter of the cataloguers') (Revelli, 2004), Carlo Revelli recalls Michael Gorman and Pat Oddy (Gorman and Oddy, 1993), who, in 1993, pointed out that cataloguing and classification require today a higher professional quality than in the past. The reason is the multiplication of media and formats and, above all, the need for greater attention in understanding the data, greater precision in the preparation of adequate records and greater functionality in creating methods for retrieving bibliographic information.

Cataloguing and managing catalogues, once an essential part of librarian training, have become more complex processes. This, however, Revelli comments, does not justify the outsourcing of the service with the consequent 'slaughter of the cataloguers' inside the library and the impoverishment of the quality of the catalogue. This is not due to the outsourcing itself but to the underfunding of a service requiring professionalism and continuity from the operators over time. The problem to be considered is the change taking place in the labour market: highly professional companies ensure flawless work, but the library needs to maintain part of the service with a solid core of librarians skilled to govern overall design and architecture.

Luigi Crocetti, in *AACR2 Italian Edition*, mentions and dismisses a bad omen:

The voices of the prophets who announced, because of the advent of machines, if not the death of cataloguing, at least its progressive decline in importance, have become increasingly dim and this activity, not only in libraries but in the entire information world, has been confirmed as the fundamental, basic activity, without which nothing can be built. On the other hand, the prophecy was correct if intended in the sense of the gradual decrease of employees, as it has happened in agriculture.

(Crocetti, 2014, 352)

Today, technology is an essential part of cataloguing (consisting of a cultural component and a technique). It allows the library to offer the reader increasingly functional and effective services integrated into the web world. Metadata have been a reality for at least 15 years in the Northern European, American, Canadian, Australian and other library contexts.

2.8 How catalogues have to change to be of the web and not just on the web

In the last 20 years there has been a dramatic change in the field of library and information science (LIS) due to the explosion of the library organism, a growing organism by definition, as the fifth Ranganathan law of librarianship stated. There are many new areas into which librarianship is moving and cataloguing undoubtedly is one of the areas where the most radical transformations have taken place on a practical and theoretical level. The expanding bibliographic universe and the migration of most bibliographic research and editorial production activities from the analogue to the digital context explain this tendency.

There are several contributions to the theoretical foundations of cataloguing and studies (e.g. Dunsire and Willer, 2013; Dunsire, 2020) about the transformations that are reshaping cataloguing in our times. One such contribution is Barbara B. Tillett's doctoral thesis, *Bibliographic Relationships: toward a conceptual structure of bibliographic information used in cataloging* (Tillett, 1987; Ghiringhelli and Guerrini, 2020), which represents the first exhaustive and essential analysis of the bibliographic universe (Morse, 2012) that focuses on bibliographic relationships. The pioneering work carried out by Tillett between 1981 and 1987 is in two parts: an analytical study and an empirical study. In the analytical study the author, through an examination of Anglo-American cataloguing codes, creates a taxonomy of bibliographic relationships in which seven categories are identified. For each identified category, Tillett outlines the history of the main linking devices used in catalogues. The empirical study was conducted by Tillett in order to evaluate the extent of bibliographic relationships as reflected through their frequency of occurrence in the machine-readable database (MARC) of the Library of Congress during the period between 1968 and July 1986. Bibliographic relationships played a central role in the development of the conceptual model FRBR, Functional Requirements for Bibliographic Records, which, in turn, is at the base of ICP, International Cataloguing Principles of 2009, and of RDA, Resource Description and Access, that devotes a large part of the text to entities, attributes and specially to bibliographic relationships. The theoretical results of Barbara

Tillett's doctoral dissertation build the fundamental basis for any scientific study on the entities, attributes, and relationships of bibliographic resources.

Theoretical reflection reached its peak with FRBR, issued by IFLA in 1998. The new philosophy of cataloguing stems from the desire to design user-friendly tools for research of resources, suitable for the digital age in terms of structure, language and use. It tends to integrate the data traditionally typical of the catalogue into the web to make them fully indexable by search engines. This integration among catalogues, databases, institutional and subject repositories, reference works and encyclopedias is a guiding motif recurring in contemporary library literature.

On the Record is an important report of the Library of Congress Working Group on the Future of Bibliographic Control published in 2008.[13] It refers to the need to transform textual description into machine-usable datasets. It aims to make data elements uniquely identifiable within the digital information context and to ensure data compatibility with web technologies and standards, using a language that is transversal and interoperable across the web. Karen Coyle, one of the report's consultants, stated that data must be *of the web and not just on the web*. The phrase has been proposed by the author in so many essays that it has become attached to her name.[14] The decisive point is the remark that the data produced by libraries – the catalogues – are on the web, but isolated from the web, that is, they are on the deep, closed web, isolated from the surface, open web.

Many bibliographic data are not reachable by search engines; thus library data remain invisible to users searching for information on the web. This situation affects all institutions that have developed databases with specific formats (such as anagraphic, geographical, statistical and scientific archives). It is therefore necessary to use standards that are interoperable with the web and with data producers from different domains, either public or private.

Hence a question arises that represents a work perspective: how to modify the catalogues so that they are *of* the web and not only *on* the web?

According to *On the Record*, this goal is achievable by:

- transforming the textual description into a set of data (dataset) presented in a structured form, usable for automatic processes by machines
- making the data uniquely identifiable within the context of the web, through unique and persistent identifiers, readable, interpretable and reusable by a machine. URIs are of crucial importance, because they give a unique and reliable name to the entities present on the web
- ensuring the compatibility of data with web technologies and standards using a transversal and interoperable language appropriate to the web.

Contemporary metadata creation confirms the need for librarians to possess a vast cultural background and the development of diversified skills related to computer science and the use of the language of the web (Malmsten, 2012). In fact, information technology is an essential discipline for the management of the library. Today's Integrated Library System (ILS) supports all library procedures.

Technology, in the original sense of the term (from the Greek (*tekne-logia*, 'treatise on an art') has always influenced or even conditioned the opening of new, previously unimaginable, avenues for librarianship. In the digital age, the IT framework affects the development and definition of bibliographic models, standards and catalogue's structure, proposed today as *resource discovery tools*.

2.9 New discovery tools: data.bnf.fr

In the space of a few years, the discovery tools of bibliographic information and resources have changed. An example is data.bnf.fr,[15] a project carried out by the Bibliothèque nationale de France. Users can search in different catalogues and databases and consult the Gallica digital library through a single access point. Once logged in, users can directly access the digital resources, available for free and open access. It is a project, imitated by other European national libraries, transforming the catalogue (a term absent in the title of the French project) into something different, provisionally named (since 2012) *Des fiches de référence sur les auteurs, les œuvres et les thèmes*. This is a product configured as a navigable multimedia encyclopedia.

Des fiches de référence adopts Semantic Web tools, being part of a linked open data project. The ability to browse by author, work and subject within data.bnf.fr lets you perceive how the catalogue of the future could be. For example, the page dedicated to an author presents biographical data, including his or her image (a drawing, a photo, etc.) or the cover of a significant book, as well as links allowing one to obtain the most studied among his or her works (with links to a database with the digital or digitised text). It also includes the roles performed by that person (author of music pieces, editor of texts, etc.), resources about that person, that is, of which that person is the subject, and other web resources referring to him or her, as well as works that provide critical analysis of his or her works. In short, an encyclopedic view of the person and his or her works is what is offered. In this project we see the epochal revolution, still in progress, from the specific *description* of a single resource, in the form of a record, to the identification of an *entity* (person) and the relationships with his or her works and with those of other authors.

From the catalogue conceived as a set of descriptions, we move on to a set of data (datasets) intended as structured information networks, placing the entity and its relationships at the centre.

The OPAC has evolved and been configured into an increasingly friendly and powerful tool. Two new finding tools have appeared: the *next generation catalogues* and the *discovery tools*. This is the result of a

> long digital revolution which, starting from the Eighties, has upset the librarian universe as it was known up to that moment. [...] In both cases we want to highlight the moment of break with tradition. Talking about next generation catalogues therefore serves to introduce a term in opposition to the old tools, just as talking about discovery tools refers to the development of modern research platforms with completely innovative characteristics.
>
> (Machetti, 2016, 394)

The discovery tools constitute an innovative technological solution: for each query they offer a unified response, deriving from the exploration of the catalogue and, above all, of the surrounding bibliographic universe, that is the resources that the library has acquired or to which it gives access. 'At the origin there is, in fact, the increase in digital publishing and the consequent need to manage the increasing amount of electronic resources that lead libraries to want a tool that offers them a simultaneous access', ideally to all resources. The discovery tool is 'an interface that gives to discovery a greater importance than the simple retrieval on which the previous tools were based' (Machetti, 2016, 394–5). By simulating the queries typical of search engines, they allow an integrated search of the data stored in multiple *silos* (containers), in non-related databases: OPACs, databases, institutional repositories. Silos typically are indexed with web-scale technologies, but they are not transferred on the web. They adopt the Google-like interface, which, in subsequent realisations, may 'interpret' user typing errors (hoping that they are not lesser-known names, correctly typed).

The discovery tools allow an all-encompassing search of the resources owned by a library and those to which it gives access. The search results are collected in a single screen that allows choosing those of interest among the results, a feature that previously required multiple queries in separate databases. The latest generation of discovery tools includes a software module for the systematic collection and indexing of the data present in the various silos, creating a unique resources index allowing the user to perform queries directly. What is of interest for those who carry out research, ultimately, is finding and discovering any resource that transmits an intellectual or artistic content on any medium and in any form, analogue or digital, regardless of the place where it is stored. There is an increasing discussion of web-scale discovery services, whose goal is to make the multiplicity of sources of information simultaneously available by libraries and institutions of recorded memory: catalogues, data, institutional repositories (especially if open access) and other databases are accessible through a unique access point. The transfer of data from the bibliographic silos to the web allows querying the whole network or an OPAC as may be needed. Users are enabled to carry out both exploratory and 'known item' searches. The interfaces of discovery tools are increasingly linked directly to the Library Service Platform, more and more pervasive in libraries.

3

Principles and Bibliographic Models

3.1 Bibliographic models

In *Principles, Rules, Standards and Applications* (Gorman, 1980), a report published in *AACR2 Seminar Papers* in 1980, Michael Gorman distinguished between these terms as follows: *principles* have a broad scope (Paris Principles), *standards* define a circumscribed framework (e.g. ISBD), *rules* present precise instructions (e.g. AACR) and *applications* propose local solutions and variants. By *rules*, we mean codes of cataloguing, often internationally inspired, but sometimes adjusted to meet the needs of national values and language communities.

Bibliographic models have been added to this list of terms since 1998. Developed in the computer environment and used in the librarianship field, they have been created for the purpose of understanding, describing and providing access to the bibliographic universe. They constitute a reference for those who create collections, those who elaborate descriptions and those who produce tools in order to help readers discover the resources that compose them.

One type of bibliographic model is a conceptual model. A conceptual model is by definition abstract and can be implemented with various interpretations. It expresses the meaning of concepts and terms used by experts of a *domain*, that is, a context, a pertinent field.

Models of the librarianship domain underlie the compilation of codes of cataloguing rules and metadata standards. Creating a model is affected by transformations due to constant acquisitions and innovations. The impact of technological evolution is evident when comparing the models of the FR family with IFLA LRM; the latter is specifically conceived for the Semantic Web context (Pisanski and Žumer, 2010).

Conceptual models have a historical reference in the E-R data model developed by computer scientist Peter Chen, professor at the Carnegie Mellon University, in the essay 'The Entity-Relationship Model. Toward a unified view of data' (Chen, 1976). Any Entity-Relationship (E-R) model that aims to describe a domain of knowledge has, as the main aspects of its design, *entities, attributes* and *relationships.*

Bibliographic models, standards and codes are situated on different levels. The former defines a way to interpret the bibliographic universe by providing an abstract framework in order to understand significant relationships among entities of a given environment. Standards and codes provide a set of criteria, reunified – according to Lubetzky – around principles of recognition (and consequent treatment) of conflicts arising from particular *bibliographic situations.* Today these situations have increased as the bibliographic universe presents a greater complexity than in the past due to the growing diversification and the vastness of data on the web (Delsey, 1982).

3.2 Paris Principles

In the mid-20th century, the need for an international comparison of cataloguing codes and relative national traditions led to the organisation of the International Conference on Cataloguing Principles (ICCP), held in Paris, at the UNESCO headquarters in 1961. That Paris meeting was preceded by four international meetings in Paris, London, Moscow and Montreal. The conference was motivated by the intention of creating a shared meeting ground, limited to the choice and shape of the author's catalogue headings. The leading cataloguing experts of the time participated in the ICCP; Seymour Lubetzky was the scientific director. At the conclusion of the work, the *Statement of Principles* was published, drafted mainly by Lubetzky, Eva Verona, Arthur H. Chaplin and Leonard J. Jolley.

Other authorities, such as Ranganathan and Ákos Domanovsky, remained, as the aim of ensuring uniformity of cataloguing practice and theory at an international level essentially implied privileging the bibliographic tradition of the West or, more precisely, of parts of Europe, USA and Canada.

The Paris Principles, as they are commonly known, do not concern the whole cataloguing process, but only the choice and form of entries, which at the time were considered the most important part of the catalogue card. Later, 'description' was discussed at the International Meeting of Cataloguing Experts (IMCE), held in Copenhagen in 1969 (Bourne, 1992), where the extension of ICCP was considered. On that occasion the 'poor relative of cataloguing' (the description), as the title of a book by Rossella Dini (1985) called it, found its rightful place.

The decision of the Principles to use the name of the author always and rigidly (thus excluding the use of the title even when better known) on the one hand seemed to:

- guarantee a high degree of homogeneity and consistency in the structure of the catalogue; and
- spare the cataloguer sometimes difficult decisions, such as when to choose the author and when to choose the title.

On the other hand, it removed from the catalogue and the cataloguer the necessary flexibility. Who, in fact, will look for *Cinderella* through the name of its author, famous but yet unknown to most? In this case, the title is undoubtedly the most reliable element for finding the work.

In Paris, *formal access points* (Convention; Conference, etc.) are overcome by recognising legitimacy only of the main heading, that is, the author or title. Given, however, that the bibliographic universe is characterised by conflicts, the use of title is always necessary where the existence of a conflict is noticed. The *Statement of Principles* is divided into 12 points. The two purposes of the catalogue are stated at the beginning of the text:

- the catalogue should be an efficient instrument for ascertaining whether the library contains a particular book specified by its title and author or its title alone
- the catalogue informs which works by a particular author and which editions of a particular work are in the library.

These clear definitions are the core of the Principles: they have an original reference in Charles A. Cutter's *Rules for a Dictionary Catalogue* (Cutter, 1876). Using contemporary language, we could assert that it represents the implicit definition of an ontology: work, edition and author.

The Paris Principles represent a landmark in the history of cataloguing, a crucial step towards the worldwide harmonisation of cataloguing practices; they are the culmination of a reflection that began in 1941 with *The Crisis in Cataloging* by Andrew D. Osborn (Osborn, 1941). The Paris Principles have been considered the reference for drafting cataloguing codes, starting with AACR in 1967 to RICA in 1979.

3.3 ICP

At the beginning of the 21st century, IFLA produced a new statement of principles (published in 2009) applicable to online library catalogues and beyond. [...] The 2009 Statement of Principles replaced and explicitly broadened the scope of the Paris Principles from just textual resources to all types of resources, and from just the choice and form of entry to all aspects of bibliographic and authority data used in library catalogues.

Thus begins the *Statement of International Cataloguing Principles* (ICP, 2016; Creider, 2009, 583–9). ICP is the outcome of an international survey promoted by IFLA Meetings of Experts on an International Cataloguing Code (IME ICC), launched in Frankfurt in 2003, with the aim to:

- develop a draft of international cataloguing principles, applicable to the contemporary cataloguing environment that could integrate or replace the Paris Principles
- bring together and harmonise the different international cataloguing codes
- formulate recommendations for a future international cataloguing code or a set of common rules addressed to the drafters of national cataloguing codes.

Also in 2003, a first draft of the Statement, known as ICP or Frankfurt Principles, was published, laying the foundations for a set of cataloguing principles with the aim of extending its contents beyond library catalogues, involving archives and museums. The amendments to the text were submitted to several meetings of IME ICC: Buenos Aires, Argentina, in 2004 (Latin American and Caribbean countries), Cairo, Egypt, in 2005 (North African and Middle Eastern countries), Seoul, Korea, in 2006 (Asian countries) and Pretoria, South Africa, in 2007 (sub-Saharan African countries). During the 2008 IFLA Congress in Québec, Canada, the Committee met in order to re-examine the comments received after the global revisions of ICP. In mid-September 2008, another draft of the Principles was sent to the participants of IME ICC for further comments and on 18 December 2008 the final draft was transmitted. The ICP text was published online in February 2009 and in a printed version in August 2009 and was presented at the IFLA 2009 Conference in Milan, Italy, with the title *Statement of International Cataloguing Principles*.

ICP intends to serve the interest of the users of every country (and not only of those of western culture) and to expand the boundaries of cataloguing to include all the possible resources held by archives, libraries, museums and other cultural institutions of recorded memory.

The *Principles*, in accordance with FRBR, state that the catalogue is an effective and efficient instrument that enables the user to:

- *find* the entities that correspond to the search criteria
- *identify* an entity
- *select* access to the entity described
- *obtain access* to an item; and
- *navigate* among the bibliographic information.

This statement covers:

1   Scope
2   General Principles
3   Entities, Attributes and Relationships
4   Objectives and Functions of the Catalogue
5   Bibliographic Description
6   Access Points
7   Searching (IFLA, 2009a).

The 2009 edition was followed by the publication of the *Statement of International Cataloguing Principles: 2016 edition* (with minor revisions in 2017) (ICP, 2016). The 2016 edition 'takes into consideration new categories of users, the open access environment, the interoperability and the accessibility of data, features of discovery tools and the significant change of user behaviour in general.'[16] The 2016 Statement follows the same points as the 2009 edition and likewise 'builds on the great cataloguing traditions of the world, as well as on the conceptual models in the IFLA Functional Requirements family'. Footnote 3 in the Statement specifies the authors that represent the great cataloguing traditions of the world:

> Cutter, Charles A., *Rules for a dictionary catalog*, 4th ed., rewritten. Washington, D.C., US Government Printing Office, 1904; Ranganathan, S. R., *Heading and canons*, Madras [India], S. Viswanathan, 1955; Lubetzky, Seymour, *Principles of Cataloging. Final Report*. Phase I: *Descriptive Cataloging*, Los Angeles, Calif.: University of California, Institute of Library Research, 1969

However, the footnote represents surprising absences, starting with Panizzi, the Prussian tradition and several other significant cataloguing traditions of the world, including Àkos Domanovzsky and Eva Verona. Hopefully, these omissions will be corrected in future editions of the principles, as they were certainly included by the participants in the 2003–2007 worldwide meetings.

Scope of the 2016 edition of ICP: compared to the 2009 edition, which attempted to apply the principles also to archives and museums, the 2016 version takes a more specifically library-oriented approach, as can be seen in its Section 1. 'They apply to bibliographic and authority data and consequently to current library catalogues, bibliographies and other datasets created by libraries. They aim to provide a consistent approach to descriptive and subject cataloguing of bibliographic resources of all kinds'. Section 2.1 defines the term *user* as embracing anyone who searches the catalogue and uses the bibliographic and/or authority data. Subsequently, the principles enumerated in 2009 and discussed by Svenonius in *The Intellectual Foundation of Information Organization* (Svenonius, 2000, as commented on by Guerrini and Genetasio, 2012) are presented:

> *Common usage.* Vocabulary used in descriptions and access points should be in accordance with that of the majority of users
>
> *Representation.* A description should represent a resource as it appears. Controlled forms of names of persons, corporate bodies and families should be based on the way an entity describes itself. Controlled forms of work titles should be based on the form appearing on the first manifestation of the original expression. If this is not feasible, the form commonly used in reference sources should be used
>
> *Accuracy.* Bibliographic and authority data should be an accurate portrayal of the entity described
>
> *Sufficiency and necessity.* Those data elements that are required to: facilitate access for all types of users, including those with specific needs; fulfil the objectives and functions of the catalogue; and describe or identify entities, should be included
>
> *Significance.* Data elements should be relevant to the description, noteworthy, and allow for distinctions among entities
>
> *Economy.* When alternative ways exist to achieve a goal, preference should be given to the way that best furthers overall expediency and practicality (i.e. the least cost or the simplest approach). The description is no longer bound by the limits of space once imposed by cost-efficiency criteria due to the use of the printed records in book or card catalogues (the basis for the editing and display of the record in the first electronic catalogues): now, there is no maximum number of data to be used and the choice of the quantity of attributes for each analysed and described resource depends on the cataloguing policy of the various libraries, library systems and bibliographic agencies
>
> *Consistency and standardisation.* Descriptions and construction of access points should be standardised as far as possible to enable consistency
>
> *Integration.* The descriptions for all types of resources and controlled forms of names of all types of entities should be based on a common set of rules to the extent possible

In addition to these:

Interoperability. All efforts should be made to ensure the sharing and reuse of
bibliographic and authority data within and outside the library community. For
the exchange of data and discovery tools, the use of vocabularies facilitating
automatic translation and disambiguation is highly recommended

Openness. Restrictions on data should be minimal in order to foster transparency
and conform to Open Access principles, as declared also in the *IFLA Statement
on Open Access.* Any restriction on data access should be fully stated

Accessibility. Access to bibliographic and authority data, as well as searching device
functionalities, should comply with international standards for accessibility as
recommended in the *IFLA Code of Ethics for Librarians and other Information
Workers*

Rationality. The rules in a cataloguing code should be defensible and not arbitrary
(ICP, 2016, 5–6).

Regarding the bibliographic description, ICP 2016 states that a separate
bibliographic description should be created for each manifestation and should
be based on the item as representative of the manifestation. Descriptive data
should be based on an internationally agreed standard which, for the
community of libraries, is ISBD. Descriptions may be at several levels of
completeness, depending on the purpose of the catalogue.

ICP distinguishes between *controlled access points* (subject to authority
control) and *uncontrolled access points* (not subject to authority control): the
Principles specify that only the former should be provided for the authorised
and variant forms of names for such entities as persons, families, corporate
bodies, works, expressions, manifestations, items and themas (that is, any
entity used as a subject of a work). Controlled access points provide the
consistency needed for collocating the bibliographic data for sets of
resources. The authorised access point for the name of an entity should be
registered as authority data together with the identifiers for the entity and
the variant forms of the name. An authorised access point may be used as a
default form for displays in the catalogue. If the original language and script
are not used in the catalogue, the authorised access point may be based on
forms found on manifestations or in reference sources in one of the languages
or script best suited to the users of the catalogue.

The Principles subsequently define *objectives* and *functions of the
catalogue*: it should be an effective and efficient instrument that enables a
user:

– *to find* bibliographic resources in a collection as the result of a search using
   attributes or relationships of the entities, that is, to find a single resource or
   sets of resources representing:

- all resources realizing the same work
- all resources embodying the same expression
- all resources exemplifying the same manifestation
- all resources associated with a given person, family or corporate body
- all resources on a given thema
- all resources defined by other criteria (language, place of publication, publication date, content form, media type, carrier type, etc.), usually as a secondary refinement of a search result
- *to identify* a bibliographic resource or agent (that is, to confirm that the described entity corresponds to the entity sought or to distinguish between two or more entities with similar characteristics)
- *to select* a bibliographic resource that is appropriate to the user's needs (that is, to choose a resource that meets the user's requirements with respect to medium, content, carrier, etc. or to reject a resource as being inappropriate to the user's needs)
- *to acquire or obtain access to an item described* (that is, to provide information that will enable the user to acquire an item through purchase, loan, etc. or to access an item electronically through an online connection to a remote source); or to access, acquire or obtain authority data or bibliographic data
- *to navigate and explore* within a catalogue, through the logical arrangement of bibliographic and authority data and the clear presentation of relationships among entities beyond the catalogue, to other catalogues and in non-library contexts

(ICP, 2016, 10–11).

ICP concludes by stating that the

access points
- provide reliable retrieval of bibliographic and authority data and their associated bibliographic resources
- collocate and limit search results

(ICP, 2016, 11).

Data should be open and searchable even by non-library devices in order to increase interoperability and reuse. Essential access points are those based on the main attributes and relationships of each entity in a bibliographic description. Essential access points in bibliographic data include:

- authorised access point for the name of the creator or first-named creator of the work when more than one is named

- authorised access point for the work/expression
- title proper or supplied title for the manifestation
- dates of publication or issuance of the manifestation
- subject access points and/or classification numbers for the work
- standard numbers, identifiers and 'key titles' for the described entity.[17]

Essential access points in authority data include:

- authorised name of the entity
- variant names and variant forms of name for the entity
- identifiers for the entity
- controlled names (e.g. subject access points and/or classification numbers) for the work (IFLA, 2016, 11–12).

The final section of the ICP 2016 edition is devoted to *data retrieval*:

> when searching retrieves a large number of bibliographic data with the same access point, results should be displayed in a logical order convenient to the catalogue user, preferably according to a standard relevant to the language and script of the access point. The user should be able to choose among different criteria: date of publication, alphabetical order, relevance ranking. If possible, preference should be given to a display showing entities and the relationships among them
>
> (ICP, 2016, 12).

An extensive glossary provides definitions of the terms, followed by an appendix with the terms no longer used in favour of new ones, for example uniform title and heading (Guerrini, 2009).

At the 2019 IFLA Congress in Athens, the Cataloguing Section included 'maintaining consistency of standards (structural revision of ICP)' among the four main commitments of their Action plan 2019–2021.[18] The intention is to redraft the text of the principles within the context of the Semantic Web.[19]

3.4 FRBR

Functional Requirements for Bibliographic Records (FRBR) was published in 1998 by the IFLA Universal Bibliographic Control and International MARC Programme. The initiative started within IFLA as a result of resolutions from the Seminar on Bibliographic Records held in Stockholm in 1990 (Seminar on Bibliographic Records, 1992). Terms of reference for the study group were approved at the IFLA Conference in New Delhi in 1992 and the resulting

Study Group appointed consultants who wrote the report. The consultants were originally Elaine Svenonius (University of California, Los Angeles), Ben Tucker (Library of Congress), Barbara Tillett (University of California, San Diego and later Library of Congress) and Tom Delsey (National Library of Canada). However, Ben Tucker soon retired and withdrew from the group. Later Beth Dulabahn, also from the Library of Congress, joined the consultants. The conception and development of the model were influenced by work on conceptual models conducted by the Library of Congress and the National Library of Canada, which also informed the aforementioned PhD dissertation *Bibliographic Relationships* by Tillett, in which the author analysed the bibliographic relationships of MARC records in the Library of Congress catalogue.

The FRBR Final Report highlights a profound crisis in cataloguing:

- rules prove to be inadequate to the change in the bibliographic universe, characterised by diversified resources in terms of contents, carriers and methods of dissemination and access, especially the new electronic resources
- catalogues are unable to represent the bibliographic universe in an optimised way, that is, to make use of the potential offered by computer and telematic systems in terms of effectiveness and cost savings.

The FRBR model aims to present the nature and requirements of the bibliographic record in relation to the various types of media, its several applications and the multiple needs of users. In particular it defines:

- the object of cataloguing, distinguishing between the tangible and intangible nature of resources
- how users read the record; rethinking description and essential data for identifying resources
- the purposes and destination of the record in light of the constant evolution of technologies.

FRBR stands as a concept map for the representation of the bibliographic universe. It makes use of the Entity-Relationship (E-R) model as it is used in all fields dealing with modelling and design of relational database systems. It defines the *user tasks* associated with the resources described in catalogues, bibliographies and other discovery tools. There are four tasks, which are defined in relation to the uses made of the data of a record:

1 to *find* entities that correspond to the user's stated search criteria, through an attribute or relationship of the entity
2 to *identify* an entity, confirming that it corresponds to the entity sought and, if necessary, distinguishing the entity from others similar
3 to *select* the entity that is appropriate to the user's needs in terms of content, carrier, format, method of utilisation
4 to *obtain* access to the entity described through loan, purchase or remote online reading.

(FRBR, 1998, 82).

FRBR considers entities the 'key objects of interest to users of bibliographic data' (IFLA, 1998, 12) and defines them by focusing on the methodologies for their research and retrieval. The model identifies ten entities divided into three groups:

Group 1: products of intellectual and/or artistic endeavour:

• Work
• Expression
• Manifestation
• Item.

Group 2: entities responsible for intellectual and/or artistic content, the physical production, the dissemination and the custodianship:

• Person
• Family (entity absent in the 1998 version)
• Corporate body.

Group 3: entities that can represent the subjects of artistic and intellectual endeavour:

• Concept
• Object
• Event
• Place.

Each entity is associated with a set of characteristics or attributes through which users formulate searches and interpret responses to those searches.

Relationships are the most important aspect of FRBR. They are divided into primary relationships (among the Group 1 entities: work, expression, manifestation and item), responsibility relationships (linking the Group 1 and Group 2 entities) and subject relationships ('has as subject'). They allow a user to identify the links among entities and, through a search, to find such things as:

- all the works of an author
- all books published in a series of monographs
- all books by a publisher
- all resources (regardless of the form) about a given subject.

FRBR's success is due to three innovative aspects:

1 the definition of users' tasks
2 the identification of the entities of interest to users
3 the re-examination of the function of bibliographic data with respect to the characterisation and identification of the description.

FRBR is the basis for the drafting of new cataloguing codes such as *Regole Italiane di Catalogazione* (REICAT) and *Resource Description and Access* (RDA).

3.5 FRAD

In 1999, the IFLA Universal Bibliographic Control and International MARC Programme (UBCIM) along with the Division of Bibliographic Control, established the IFLA Working Group on Functional Requirements and Numbering of Authority Records (FRANAR) with the aim of pursuing three objectives:

1 expand the FRBR model, defining the functional requirements of authority data
2 study the possibility of creating an International Standard Authority Data Number (ISADN) to uniquely identify controlled authority data
3 represent IFLA in its co-operation with other working groups created with the same purposes.

Functional Requirements for Authority Data (FRAD) was published in 2009 and is devoted to the creation of authority data, understood as the authorised form of the name or title of a work, combined with other elements that create access to the description. In the name, 'Data' replaces the 'Record' of the original version[20] and, above all, of *Functional Requirements for Bibliographic Records*, as a reflection of the conceptual (and therefore terminological) transformation that took place in the early years of the 21st century, with the (general) conceptual transition from 'records' to 'data'.

Compared to FRBR, FRAD adds two users' tasks:

1 *Contextualise*, i.e. place an entity in its original context
2 *Justify*, i.e. document the use of a controlled access point in one form rather than another.

The model revises the FRBR entities for authority data and creates: *family, name, identifier, controlled access point, rules* and *agency*. It clarifies that relationships define the type of association that may exist between entities of Group 1 and Group 2 of FRBR.

3.6 FRSAD

Functional Requirements for Subject Authority Data (FRSAD) was published by IFLA in 2010; the model defines the FRBR Group 3 entities: *concept, object, event* and *place*. Its aims are:

- to provide a clearly defined, structured frame of reference for relating the data that are recorded in subject authority records to the needs of the users of that data
- to assist in an assessment of the potential for international sharing and use of subject authority data both within the library sector and beyond.

The model adds the users' task *explore*, that is, the use of data in order to understand the relationships between a subject domain and its subject strings. It also adds the entities *thema* (as seen above, any entity used as a subject of a work) and *nomen* (any sign or sequence of signs by which a thema is known, referred to, or addressed as), defining their *attributes*. Finally, FRSAD establishes the relationships between different entities such as work and thema, thema and nomen and those between entities of the same type: thema and thema, nomen and nomen.

3.7 FRBRoo

FRBR, FRAD and FRSAD are characterised by a bibliocentric view. The need to harmonise the conceptual model of bibliographic, archival and especially museum resources was first expressed in 2000, on the occasion of the European Library Automation Group's (ELAG) 24th Library Systems Seminar in Paris. In 2003 the International Working Group on FRBR/CIDOC CRM Harmonisation was established, with the aim to:

- rewrite FRBR by adopting concepts and terminology provided by the Comité International pour la DOCumentation – Conceptual Reference Model (CIDOC CRM)
- align the two models and possibly even merge them.

FRBR-object oriented version 1.0: *A Conceptual Model for Bibliographic Information in Object-oriented Formalism* (FRBRoo) was published in 2009 (available in version 2.4 updated to 2016). FRBR entities are expanded by identifying subclasses, each with specific properties. The model, given its considerable complexity, has had a limited reception (Le Boeuf, 2009).

3.8 IFLA LRM

IFLA LRM (Library Reference Model) was published in 2017, after more than five years of work. It is a high-level conceptual reference model resulting from the harmonisation of FRBR, FRAD and FRSAD. The model aims to make explicit general principles governing the logical structure of bibliographic information, without making presuppositions about how that data might be stored in any particular system or application. Like the model from which it results and which it replaces, IFLA LRM provides an E-R structure that, as such, presents three fundamental modelling elements: *entities*, *attributes* and *relationships*. As with previous models, at the basis of the definition are user tasks, not necessarily sequential, nor all always included – indeed, they may intertwine variously or be independent of each other. The user tasks are:

1 *Find*: to bring together information about one or more resources of interest by searching on any relevant criteria
2 *Identify*: to clearly understand the nature of the resources found and to distinguish between similar resources
3 *Select*: to determine the suitability of the resources found and to be enabled to either accept or reject specific resources
4 *Obtain*: access to the content of the resource
5 *Explore*: to discover resources using the relationships between them.

Note here that the ICP user task of 'navigate' has become 'explore'.
IFLA LRM incorporates the entities of the FRBR Group 1, with changes in the definition in order to make them more independent from each other. Group 2 entities *Family* and *Corporate body* are no longer autonomous and are subsumed in the new entity, *Collective agent*. Group 3 entities, *Concept*, *Object* and *Event*, are declared deprecated; the entity *Place* is redefined and *Time-span* is added. *Res*, using the IFLA LRM definition, is the top entity of

the model that includes all the other entities. Another new entity is *Nomen*, which merges the entities *Name* and *Nomen* from FRAD and FRSAD with a substantial change: in IFLA LRM, the entity *Nomen* becomes a relationship, while in FRBR it was an attribute.

It is worth noting that there are many terms taken from Latin, such as *Nomen*, *Res* (that is, any entity in the universe of discourse), and *Thema*. Latin terms would have been chosen to signify new concepts; as these concepts are new, common, frequently used and plain, original terms cannot be used (Bianchini and Guerrini, 2018).

In brief, IFLA LRM includes *entities*, *attributes* and *relationships* as follows:

- 11 *entities*, organised in superclasses and subclasses that determine the structure of the model:
  – One top-level entity (*Res*)
  – Eight second-level entities (*Work, Expression, Manifestation, Item, Agent, Nomen, Place* and *Time-span*)
  – Two third-level entities (*Person* and *Collective Agent*, subclasses of the entity *Agent*).
- 37 *attributes*, i.e. data that provide information about the characteristics of instances of an entity. They can be represented in two ways: by a sequence of symbols, i.e. a literal (a string or number) or by URIs that point to an external source. Some attributes can be represented in both ways, others only as a literal or only as a URI.
- 36 *relationships*, i.e. the properties that connect instances of entities. They are defined by an entity that functions as a domain, that is, the starting point, the source of the relationship, associated with an entity representing its range, i.e. the target of the relationship, the point of arrival. The relationship model provides four types:
  1 *basic relationships*: they are the core of the model and are those between works, expressions, manifestations and items
  2 *responsibility relationships*: these relationships all hold between the entity agent (or by extension either of its subclasses) and works, expressions, manifestations and items. These relationships capture responsibility for the processes of creation, manufacture, distribution, ownership or modification
  3 *subject relationships*: these relationships link work to the Res which is the subject of the work
  4 *appellation relationships*: these link an entity to the Nomen string.

The list of attributes and relationships is not exhaustive and lends itself to further expansion.

Another important change is the *representative expression attribute* (in the sense of *typical expression*), a new attribute considered essential to characterise the Work. The values are inferred from the reference expression of the Work; its function, Pat Riva explains (Riva, 2016), is the identification of some significant attributes – such as intended audience, language, key and medium of performance, musical scale – in order to measure the distance between different expressions of the same work. FRBR, on the other hand, treats all expressions of a work as equivalent. The concept, hypothesised by Pino Buizza at the FRBR Seminar (Guerrini, 2000), is straightforward but of complex application and the model cannot and will not represent all the particularities, which it leaves to implementation in cataloguing practices. For a textual work, for example, the representative expression attribute will be the language, with the value inferred from the original expression, if possible; e.g. English for James Joyce's *Ulysses*. Having defined this, all translations into numerous languages – that is, with a different value for the language attribute – are distinguished as non-representative expressions, compared to the English edition that shares the language.

Therefore, 'representative expressions' of the same language are considered, e.g:

- the first version of the story of Pinocchio, published under the title 'La Storia di un Burattino' ('The Story of a Puppet') in the magazine *Giornale per i Bambini* (*Children's Newspaper*), in 30 episodes published in 26 issues from 7 July 1881 to 25 January 1883.
- the first edition of Collodi's book *Le Avventure di Pinocchio* (*The Adventures of Pinocchio*), published in Florence, Italy, by Paggi in 1883. This book presents the final draft of the story.

Both expressions (both texts), although with different text and with different titles, are the reference for the subsequent editions in Italian and for the translation of the story of Pinocchio into countless languages.

Compared to FRBR, IFLA LRM introduces some key concepts:

1 *Hierarchy*: the model has a hierarchical structure. An entity can be declared a superclass of other entities, which consequently will be its subclasses. Each instance of the subclass entity is an instance of the superclass. Attributes and relationships also have a hierarchical structure.
2 *Inheritance*: relationships and attributes defined for a superclass entity are inherited by subclasses, but the reverse direction does not hold.

3 *Disjointness*: between different entities some bonds can exist, but generally, the entities declared in the model are defined as 'disjoint', to indicate that the entities placed in the same hierarchical level cannot have common instances. For example, a place cannot be a time-span.
4 *Cardinality*: can be 1 to M (M meaning many) and implies that each instance of the domain entity can be connected to more than one instance of the entity to which it is associated by the relationship (and vice versa); or can be M to M, meaning that each instance can be connected to multiple instances of the entity by the relationship.[21]

Finally, IFLA LRM models *aggregates* and *serials*.

An aggregate is defined as a manifestation embodying multiple expressions. Three distinct types of aggregates exist:

1 Collections of expressions: anthologies, monographic series, issues of serials, multiple novels published together in a single volume, etc.
2 Aggregates resulting from augmentation: enlarged editions with notes, illustrations, etc.
3 Aggregates of parallel expressions: an original text with a translation, a multiple language work publication.

Additional text (prefaces, introductory essays, etc.) in IFLA LRM represents non-autonomous works. Their description is decided by the bibliographic agency creating the data and is motivated by context and user needs.

A *serial* (a journal, a newspaper, a series of monographs) is a resource published in consecutive parts, that is usually numbered and has no predetermined conclusion. Serials are complex constructs that combine whole/part relationships and aggregation relationships. In fact:

• the complete serial manifestation has a whole/part relationship to its individual issues published over time
• each individual issue is an aggregate of articles even though there are serials that can occasionally have issues consisting of only one article.

IFLA LRM is situated in the context of the Semantic Web and linked data technology, reflecting the process of atomisation of data in the digital environment. The model, in this regard, analyses the data and no longer the record (Riva, 2016; 2018; Guerrini and Sardo, 2018).

In conclusion, IFLA LRM describes the bibliographic universe by attempting to facilitate the definition of necessary and sufficient data to describe resources within the philosophy of the Semantic Web and linked data technology. The entities, their attributes and their relationships are defined with data built according to the logic of RDF triples. This solution enables semantic interoperability between applications that share information on the web.

3.9 Family of works

The bibliographic universe is populated by many objects that contribute to making it articulate. The complexity increases if we think that certain works are derivatives of others. There are many examples. From the novel *The Name of the Rose* by Umberto Eco, published in Italy by Bompiani in 1980, the film of the same name was made in 1986, directed by Jean-Jacques Annaud and with a screenplay by Andrew Birkin, Gérard Brach, Howard Franklin and Alain Godard. A *derivative work* such as the film, therefore, is a different work from the novel, with a translation of the plot (partially revised) in an artistically different canon from that of the written text. Other products inspired by the novel are also new works: the television series, the comic documentary, the radio play and the theatrical performance. Scripts for films, theatrical representations, remakes and parodies of various kinds of *Alice in Wonderland* by Lewis Carroll have all been written. There are translations of Virgil's *Aeneid* in various languages, as well as prose transcriptions and annotated editions. There are condensed versions and updated and enlarged editions of many manuals. There are facsimile reproductions of many manuscripts and rare editions. The relationships that exist and can be established among resources are inexhaustible. Abridged versions for children and young people, such as those used for language learning, represent a special case. In children's versions of *The Three Musketeers*, *Pinocchio* and the Bible, for example, if a work is abridged beyond a certain point, it becomes a mere plot – the original work is thus completely transformed into another work with little relation to the original.

Figure 3.1 opposite is important for understanding the representation of the possible variants and transformations of a work: *original work, equivalent works, equivalent expressions* and *derivative works*. The range is countless and the scheme, like any simplification, tends to be rigid, but is helpful to understand the concepts.

The diagram derives from the taxonomy of bibliographic relationships by Barbara B. Tillett (published in Bean and Green, 2001), with slight variations introduced by Tillett in 2011.[22]

Reading the scheme from left to right shows a *continuum* of content relationships for the family of works. On the left are *equivalent relationships* between *different manifestations* of the same work and expression (e.g. paperback v. hardcover editions) or *different items* (e.g. different copies of

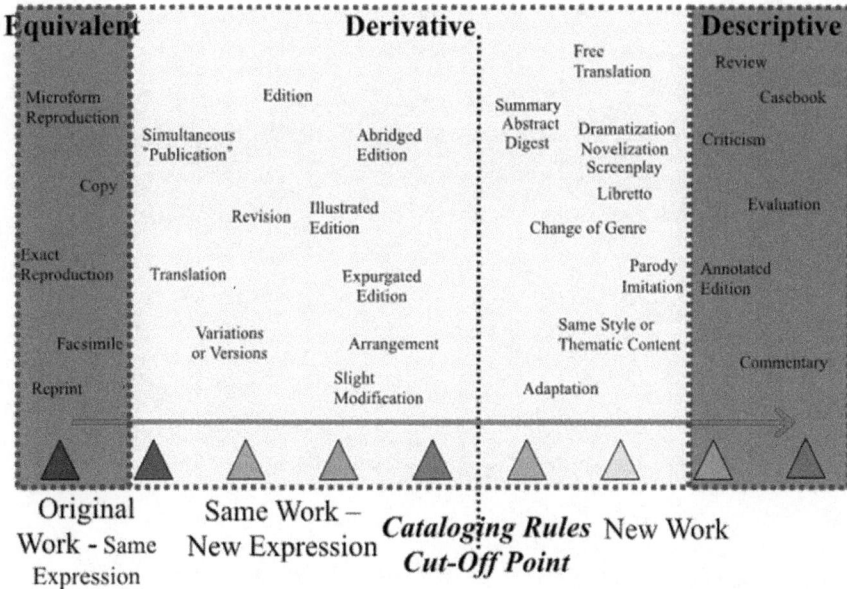

Equivalent		Derivative		Descriptive
	Edition		Free Translation	Review
Microform Reproduction		Summary Abstract Digest	Dramatization	Casebook
	Simultaneous "Publication"	Abridged Edition	Novelization Screenplay	Criticism
Copy			Libretto	Evaluation
	Revision	Illustrated Edition	Change of Genre	
Exact Reproduction	Translation	Expurgated Edition	Parody Imitation	Annotated Edition
Facsimile	Variations or Versions	Arrangement	Same Style or Thematic Content	
				Commentary
Reprint		Slight Modification	Adaptation	

Original Work - Same Expression   Same Work – New Expression   *Cataloging Rules Cut-Off Point*   New Work

Figure 3.1 *Family of works*

the same manifestation of the work). Then moving further right along the continuum, we have *derivative works* that are just slight modifications of the expression (e.g. language change, text revision, etc.). Next we come to the point where the modification of content is sufficiently major to become a *new work* (e.g. genre change, parody, etc.). Then at the right side of the continuum are *descriptive relationships* that are *new works* that reference the original work (reviews). In other words, on the left, the *equivalent works* contain the same expression of the original work (copies, reproductions, facsimiles). Once a change in content is introduced, as in a second edition or a translation, there is a *new expression of the same work*. Towards the centre are the *expressions derived from the work* (abridged, illustrated, and expurgated editions, musical arrangements). When crossing the dotted line of current cataloguing conventions, the work is considered a new work attributable to another author. To the right of the dotted line, then, are new works derived from the original work (adaptations, novelisation, free translations), and, still further to the right, works whose subject matter is the original work (reviews, evaluations). The term 'annotated edition' should be taken to mean a text whose focus is on commentary on the work.

4

Description of Resources

4.1 Description: a cultural and technical process

> Information to be organised needs to be described
> (Svenonius, 2000, 53)

Bibliographic models and international cataloguing principles have attempted to define bibliographic data (*description*) and authority data (*access*) precisely to organise information about the resources described.

Description is the primary procedure (in the sense that it is the procedure that is carried out first) of the cataloguing process and is foremost a *conscious interpretation* of data. It is analysis, evaluation, and reflects knowledge of what is being represented. Its object, therefore, is the resource being examined, which, in Domanovszky's words, still valid decades after their enunciation, can consist of either an *elementary object* or a *main elementary object* and *secondary object* (e.g. aggregates, attachments, supplements) (Domanovszky, 1975).

The description is aimed at the identification and characterisation of a resource, which is simultaneously a material object and an intellectual content – a dimension that has been referred to by many, including Domanovszky. Its inextricable and fascinating ontological duplicity underlies the question: 'What exactly does the catalogue describe?' The question is anything but simple and resolved. Rossella Dini writes, 'What is the object of a bibliographic description? In other words, what should a distinct bibliographic record describe? No code or cataloguing manual has ever established this.' (Dini, 1991, 135) The question still awaits a comprehensive answer, although FRBR (and later IFLA LRM) posed the problem in explicit terms and, according to Pino Buizza, studied 'the object of cataloguing in a new, dynamic way' (Buizza, 2002).

The record, hence, is *a set of data that identifies and characterises an entity*. Today, description is supported by automated processes (data capture) and will take the form of an ever-increasing enrichment of information already available on the internet. The issue of 'whom to trust' will be of vital importance. With the advancement of methods and tools based on artificial intelligence, it is conceivable that we will see a further evolution also in the field of metadata.

The faithful recording of data, i.e. how they are found on the source of information, should not be confused with a mechanical procedure. It is, rather, a method that respects how the data appear on the resource and are recorded, excluding manipulation: for example, transcribing in Latin characters or translating into English an original title in Japanese (as sometimes occurred in the past). Even abbreviations are avoided, for example, not '3. ed.' but 'third edition', not 'Houghton Mifflin Co.' but 'Houghton Mifflin Company', if it appears so on the source.

The primacy of bibliographic description, achieved with the publication of ISBD and crowned by the structure of AACR2 (both with Gorman's initial responsibility for the text), is superseded by the consideration that all entities are on the same level. The traditional record, therefore, is transformed into a dataset assembled according to different and personalised needs. The vision focused on the creation of bibliographic records is modified in favour of a method that sees the object of its interest in the identification of specific entities and, consequently, in the creation of relationships between them.

Scenario 1 outlined by Delsey in 2007 (Delsey, 2007) as one of the possible schemes of representation of the catalogues of the future provides that the description can be the result of a set of data recorded separately and assembled according to various methods and various criteria; assembled always rationally and not arbitrarily. These data represent the resource and can be combined in new aggregations with different relationships. It is a logical leap of significant scope that provides new and fruitful opportunities. The *object of description* becomes any entity of interest to the reader, e.g. the manifestation, the work, the author, a subject, etc. The reader can thus navigate a portal consisting of web pages representing the entities conceived by FRBR and developed by IFLA LRM. It opens up the possibility (already partially under way) of the transition from closed registration – that is, a registration made of individual constituent data, indivisible, tightly joined together, as is the case in current catalogues – to open data on the web; the technology of linked data is a decisive innovation in the field of global communication.

4.2 A new way to describe

The traditional cataloguing process starts from the description of an *item* considered to be one of a set of identical items. It provides the recording of descriptive elements structured in defined areas, preceded by conventional punctuation, in compliance with ISBD, *International Standard Bibliographic Description*, developed by IFLA from 1969 onwards. The record obtained is equipped with a set of elements (*headings* or *access points*) through which it becomes indexable, searchable and accessible.

Metadata do not change the process. *Identifying* and *connecting entities* correspond to the two components of traditional cataloguing: *description* and creation of *access points* for resources. Nor does it change the attitude of accuracy typical of traditional cataloguing, confirming that the cataloguer or data manager is not a transcriber of signs, but an interpreter of signs and of attributes characterising the resource. This approach helps us to understand the ambiguities that may arise in the resources. The anonymous volunteers of Wikipedia, English edition, appear to have grasped the current trends when they define cataloguing as 'the process of creating metadata that represent resources, such as books, sound recordings, moving images, etc'.[23]

In summary, the process of creating metadata consists of:

1 *identifying* entities that characterise resources
2 *connecting* the entities through relationships.

The description, or the conscious recording of a specific resource's distinctive, characterising data, has accentuated the direction towards greater granularity. This process began with the MARC Format (MAchine Readable Cataloging) in the mid-1960s. Above all, it has pursued a fragmentation of data, no longer aligned in a predetermined descriptive sequence within the frame of a record, but formalised and made independent from the context in order to be used and merged in different ways.

4.3 Object of the description
According to the terms of a discussion between Seymour Lubetzky and Eva Verona (Verona, 1959), description has as its object:

- the *bibliographic unit* – the resource as a physical object in its dimension as a vehicle for texts – and
- the *literary unit* – the content articulated in a particular linguistic and textual form (complete works, parts of works, etc.).

The descriptive process begins with the *copy in hand* – an instance of the specific resource analysed – treated as *evidence* of a whole, as a manifestation of an expression of a work in its historicity (historical authenticity) and relationships. Compared to a national bibliographic agency, a library accounts for the particular resource it owns (or gives remote access to a resource) as part of its collection. Resources can be published as finished (a single book) or as destined to be completed according to a predetermined schedule (an encyclopedia planned for 40 volumes) or to continue without having established a termination (a periodical). Resources can also be continuously updated (technical rules, evolving manuals, wiki comments, websites, blogs, online newspapers, etc.).

The description identifies and characterises the resource as a *carrier* and as a *message*. It selects those peculiar data that *characterise* the resource for the entities Item, Manifestation and (above all) Work, through its attributes and, if helpful or necessary, through other information defined by the literary tradition. The description, ultimately, makes a definite distinction of one resource from another, highlighting the contrasting data of different manifestations. A resource can be identified by a statement of edition that requires a separate description from a resource with another edition. The description achieves its objective when it creates a correspondence between the metadata and data present on the resource. It reconstructs the *individuality* of each resource by means of the distinctive characteristics concerning:

1 the work (what it is, who created it)
2 the expression (e.g. how the content is conveyed in terms of language; form of performance or presentation; what means are used to express the content/work; what text, if written words – original, abridged, modified, translated; is it musically arranged?)
3 the manifestation (e.g. what form of packaging, who produced it, who published it and when)
4 the item (e.g. peculiarities of the copy, the instance analysed) (Smiraglia, 2001; 2018; Yee, 1994; 1995).

4.4 Resource analysis: the bibliographic analysis

Analytical procedures are performed at a critical moment in determining the entities of a resource and in identifying the entities responsible for its intellectual or artistic content. Achieving a good result requires understanding what the resource is and posing questions related to its editorial presentation, content and responsibility.

Once the resource has been analysed from a formal, literary and conceptual point of view (the entire process is called bibliographic analysis), each datum is assembled in a dataset, within a database. The recording of the data reflects the process of atomisation typical of the digital context.

The first and basic step of the descriptive process is the *analysis of the resource*: the *bibliographic analysis*. Bibliographic analysis consists in the choice of necessary and sufficient data for identification and characterisation of a resource. It is an autonomous process at the same time that it is conditioned by the type of indexing established. As Fabrizio Leonardelli suggests, just as a land surface is surveyed and represented in different ways in different types of maps (political, geological, physical, climatic, hydrological, seismic, etc.), so a resource is analysed and represented in different ways in different types of descriptions. The quantity of data recorded and assembled varies according to the context for which the recording is intended, the audience and other purposes. FRBR refers to a *minimum level*, that is, minimum data that must appear in the records produced by national bibliographies. Consequently, the descriptive analysis can lead to different outcomes for the same resource or resources with the same characteristics. In fact, it always relates to the context for which it is intended: a specialised library, a general library, a database.

The process of bibliographic analysis consists of three autonomous and at the same time interrelated parts:

1 formal analysis
2 literary analysis
3 conceptual analysis.

1. *Formal analysis* (analysis of the resource as a carrier) aims to understand how the resource appears as an object characterised by distinctive identification data. It examines the labels placed, usually, in conventional parts (for a book: title page, verso of title page, colophon, cover, spine, etc.). It evaluates the nature and meaning of each attribute: title, title of the series, original title (in the case of a translation), author, editor, translator, illustrator, first or subsequent edition, reprint, publisher, date of publication, mode of use. It focuses first of all on the intellectual and editorial responsibilities and physical characteristics. It analyses the attributes on the sources of information (diversified by type of resource) and the role that each of them has. Formal analysis, therefore, investigates the historically determined language of self-representation of a resource that characterises its belonging to an era, to an editorial style, to a particular audience, etc. These are significant formal variables to be considered with accuracy and competence.

2. *Literary analysis* (*work analysis*) examines the resource as a product of intellectual or artistic work and considers its publishing history. The resource is always a vehicle for a specific expression of a work. For example, The *Divine Comedy* by Dante Alighieri was translated from Italian into numerous languages. In 1814 Henry Francis Cary published his version entitled *The Vision of Dante*. In addition to the title, which does not

correspond to the original, Cary replaced the third rhyme with the blank verse and the triplet division with the paragraph. In his work Cary also created links between Dante's verses and those of Chaucer and Shakespeare. In 1867 Henry Wadsworth Longfellow translated the entire poem *Divine Comedy* in three volumes, with rich appendices of judgements and illustrative materials. What difference exists between these two texts of Cary and Longfellow and all the other versions of Dante's masterpiece?

The literary analysis identifies the entities present in the resource and the peculiarities not perceived by the formal analysis (sharing, however, many points in common). The description and the creation of the access point are based on the formal and literary characteristics of the resource. Literary analysis, moreover, takes into account external sources of information, such as history of literature and science and directories, in order to:

1 identify the title by which the work is best known and commonly cited when known by various titles (including titles of translations)
2 trace the work back to its author – when possible – in cases where the name does not appear in the resource or appears with a fantasy formulation, for literary fun or fear of censorship
3 provide the record with information about the publishing history of the work that is necessary or helpful for understanding the record.

In order to make the intelligibility of the record clearer, formal data may be supplemented with data gathered from literary analysis. Nevertheless, the description does not have the purpose of literary verification: the history of a text is not necessarily represented in its manifestation and, consequently, in the record. The librarian does not provide a study of the origin of each resource described. Instead, the librarian considers verified and accessible information, as well as studies by experts and specialists. The cataloguer interprets the resources with the help of indexes and bibliographies that provide for the literary analysis; the librarian acquires information when it is appropriate to improve the intelligibility of the record. The cataloguer's work is based on a methodologically conscious understanding of the variability of the signs that characterise the manifestations; these signs, occasionally, may conceal or make unclear the texts (expressions). This conscious methodology of analysis is essential for the identification of the contents of the texts and for the determination of the resource's audience.

There are many cases in which the author appears on the title page of a book with generic, misleading or intentionally deceptive formulation. As an example, the 1817 edition of *Hymn to Neptune* appears on the title page as 'of uncertain author' ('d'incerto autore') and declares it is translated from

Greek into Italian by the Italian poet Giacomo Leopardi, who in fact was the real author of *Hymn to Neptune*.

3. *Conceptual analysis* (*content analysis* or *subject analysis*) is the procedure that describes a resource in terms of its conceptual content through a process of intellectual analysis. Conceptual analysis identifies and defines the basic theme, the subject matter primarily dealt with by the work. Understanding what the work deals with is an act of knowledge; the success of the analysis is directly proportional to the competence of the cataloguer. He or she has to know well the conceptual area in which the work is placed, and the indexing language in which he/she translates the result of the conceptual analysis. The conceptual analysis concerns all methods of subject indexing; it is preliminarily influenced by the chosen strategy: should we select only macro-themes (*summarisation*) or also secondary themes? The standard ISO 5963 *Documentation. Methods for examining documents, determining their subject and selecting indexing terms* of 1985 (confirmed in 2020) recommends the examination of the resource through a technical reading focused on some significant elements, such as:

1 the *title*, important for understanding the subject, but in some cases misleading or irrelevant (the subtitle can sometimes make up for a cryptic title)
2 the *abstract*, useful to provide an idea of the content
3 the *table of contents*, useful when it is detailed
4 *beginnings and conclusions*, useful for statements of purpose and research methodology
5 *illustrations*, tables and diagrams
6 *highlighted words or sentences*, useful because they signal concepts that the author or editor deems particularly important
7 *notes and bibliography*, useful to clarify and deepen the context of the topic.

4.5 Sources of information
The *paratext* constitutes a key source for the description of resources.[24] It can be defined as the set of textual and graphic elements surrounding a text that serves to present it in the context of its distribution, reception and use. The French literary critic Gérard Genette discussed it widely in his famous book *Seuils* (Genette, 1987).

The sources of information vary according to the type of resource described and the type of description made (e.g. an analytical description). However, the main source always is the resource itself. Only when data are gathered from the resource is it guaranteed that the data are objective. If, in fact, the data are gathered from an external source (e.g. an encyclopedia) there is a mediation by an editorial staff. It is precisely for this reason that, among the sources of information, the resource itself has explicit priority over other external sources. The resource has always had priority over external sources; standards now explicitly state this priority. In the past, for example, data obtained from the cover rather than from the title page of a volume were considered integrative information. Yet for many readers the cover is a more significant source than the title page (which is a conventional source, used by cataloguers): the cover is what one sees on a bookstore shelf. The preferred source of information is, therefore, a privileged source that summarises many of the resource's self-descriptive data, but it is not an exclusive source – the presentation format, storage medium, slipcase and accompanying materials (e.g. a box with ten compact discs) are equally important.

If a resource is in *tête-bêche* format (e.g. a text in English and Italian, presented front to back), the preferred source is the one with data in the language or script of the bibliographic agency producing the description.

For motion pictures, the preferred source of information is the title frame(s) or the title screen(s); otherwise, the source is a title on a label printed or permanently applied to the carrier (e.g. on the film canister, on the DVD or CD).

The preferred source of information for online resources consists of textual content or textually embedded metadata that includes a title (e.g. metadata embedded in a MPEG video file).

Data are obtained from a source external to the resource (if such exists) only if those necessary for its identification are unavailable from an internal source.

There are resource types that usually do not have the descriptive data necessary for their identification, such as photographs. In this case, it is unnecessary to state that the data have been obtained from an external source, as it is understood.

4.6 Main sources of information to describe a book

Title page. It is the place (the page) where the title appears. In the case of a modern book, it is the page (in some cases two pages) located at the beginning of the text and separated from it, displaying its identifying and characterising data: the title, the author, the editor, occasionally the statement of edition, the name of the publisher and, less frequently, the place and the date of publication.

Preliminaries. Preliminaries (or preliminary pages) are the pages between the cover and the text, which include the half-title (the page preceding the title page with only the title of the work, the title and the numbering of the series) and the back of the title page.

Verso of title page. Located at the back of the title page, the verso may include such information as the original title of a translated work, the name of the translator (when not on the title page), the statement of edition, the copyright owner, the publisher's address, the International Standard Book Number (ISBN), the International Standard Serial Number (ISSN) of a series, Digital Object Identifier (DOI) – since the beginning of the 21st century – and other data.

Title page substitute. It is the source that presents data usually found on the title page (e.g. the title) that is taken as the chief source of information in the absence of a title page; the *title page substitute* can be the cover, the caption, the masthead, etc.

Colophon. It is located at the end of the book; it provides information about the manufacture, the name of the printer, the place and date of printing. For some valuable books, the colophon specifies such information as the number of copies printed, the number of each copy, the type of paper and the typeface (font) used.

Spine. Information found on the spine of a book generally indicates the name of the author and the title of the resource; it may include such information as the title and numbering of the series. Data often appear in an abbreviated form compared to the formulation on the title page, for example, the author's initials followed by surname, title proper without subtitle, title of the series sometimes formulated with an abbreviation (e.g. Faber & Faber becoming ff), etc.

The websites of many publishers are a relevant source of information but, like other websites, should be considered with caution. Some are very well maintained, while others have inaccuracies and are incomplete, including, for example, the absence of the date of the successive editions of a work or the omission of the original title of a translated work.

4.7 Types of description

The purpose of description is to identify and characterise a resource. This implies identifying similarities and differences in the data. It is important, for instance, to distinguish between a bound edition and a paperback edition of a work published by the same publisher. It is even more important to identify the series of the specific edition in order not to confuse the two bibliographic objects and to favour an appropriate and coherent encounter between book and reader.

There are, schematically, three types of description that serve different purposes:

1 standard (regular)
2 diplomatic
3 specialised.

The purpose of the *standard description* is to provide a representation of the resource that contains the data deemed necessary in any context, in accordance with internationally and nationally shared norms.

In *Descriptive Bibliography* (Bowers, 1995; Tanselle, 2020), we speak of a *diplomatic description*. The diplomatic description aims to maintain substantial and strict fidelity to the form and sequence of the data as they are formulated on the sources of information. As to whether this type of imitative description translates the characteristics of a book, the Italian scholars Francesco Barberi and Luigi Balsamo are highly sceptical. Barberi states that:

> The faithful, 'diplomatic', almost facsimile transcription of a title page, whatever the accuracy and care taken in what appears to the layman to be a banal copying operation, will never translate the exact image of it, which can only be provided by the photograph: think of the form and body of the characters, abbreviations, ligatures, the particular shape of certain letters, punctuation and accents, printing errors, interlineations, excessively long titles and small ornamental marks. Even within the volume, not all the minute typographic and ornamental particularities can be detected. Even the searches that the scrupulous bibliographer undertakes in order to identify a typographer, an author or a contributor, will have a reasonable limit: what such a limit actually is, it is easier to guess than to define exactly.
>
> (Barberi, 1961, 212).

Balsamo comments that:

> Although diplomatic transcription performs very analytical tasks of information, these are still not exhaustive; for instance, with regard to the study of typefaces and illustration, such description must be completed with the support of facsimile reproductions. It follows that we cannot speak, as some wrongly do, of a 'facsimile transcription' (only a reproduction can be facsimile) or even of a 'semi-diplomatic transcription': a transcription is either diplomatic or it is not, since if absolute graphic and textual fidelity is renounced, not only does it become impossible for the reader to measure the degree of variance, but above all the guarantee of documentary fidelity, indispensable to a critical study, is eliminated.
>
> (Balsamo, 1989, 38).

Other analyses consider the material aspects of the book (paper, binding, collation) usually printed before the introduction of industrial technologies (in the early 19th century): books of antiquarian interest, rare or precious books, including those of the contemporary age.

Specialised description takes the form of an essay on the objective and conceptual aspects of the resource. It enters the field of codicological, philological or literary description in the strict sense; generally, it concerns manuscripts, ancient books (such as incunabula, 15th- and 16th-century books), and printed music. It is not uncommon for misunderstandings to arise between the librarian and the scholar, who would like, and sometimes demand, a description for research purposes. The task of the cataloguer is to record the necessary and objective data that enables the identification and characterisation of a resource. In principle, other purposes are extraneous to the cataloguer although, historically, it is librarians who have compiled, and in many cases continue to compile catalogues of manuscripts, cartographic resources and other resources that need specific expertise.

Each resource can be described according to different methodologies. The type of description is determined by the intended purpose. Standard descriptions can co-exist with specialised descriptions, if the library has the competence and strengths to do so. Indeed, a specialised library, limiting itself to a standard description, would only partially achieve its goals. Drawing up a catalogue for a thematic or special-interest collection intended for a specific public requires a study that is able to offer in-depth information, capable of evaluating and placing each resource in the bibliographical and conceptual framework of the collection and in the historical and literary context in which it was conceived, with information on the origin of the text, e.g. the purpose and audience of a pamphlet. In these cases, collaboration with scholars and the cataloguer's skills are indispensable requirements for achieving the fundamental quality of the cataloguing data.

4.8 Levels of description

There are various levels of description: from an essential record to a record with descriptive details to complex records resulting from their purposes. These can be:

- *comprehensive description*: when a multipart resource is recorded as a whole; e.g. a map consisting of several individual sheets, a discontinued journal, a collection of posters collected by a library
- *analytical description*: when a part of a resource is described individually; e.g. an essay as part of a journal or Festschrift, a volume of a three-volume biography, a single map as part of a set of maps

- *hierarchical description*: when the comprehensive description of the resource is combined with analytical descriptions of one or more parts of it.[25]

5

Access to Resources

5.1 Access: authority data

The process of description – intended as the identification of an entity through the recording of its attributes – is followed by the creation of access points; access points can be defined as links between entities based on the relationships existing among them. (Access points are discussed by ICP, FRBR – and FRAD in particular – and IFLA LRM, as we saw earlier). The access points according to ICP:

- provide reliable retrieval of bibliographic and authority data and their associated bibliographic resources
- collocate and limit search results.

Authority data, according to FRAD, is intended as the authorised form of the name or title of a work, combined with other elements that create access to the description.

The recording of descriptive data is textually faithful to their formulation on the sources of information of the resource. At the same time the authority data are structured according to the logic of the reference norms. The formulation of the access point requires an in-depth analysis of the resource that invokes the sense of the Latin verb *intelligere*, in terms of understanding exactly the meaning of the data, beyond their formulation on the source. Rossella Dini synthesised the concept: 'In short, it is a matter of establishing an organisation for bibliographical information that reveals their reciprocal relationships in terms of their intellectual content and genesis' (Dini, 1991, 144).

The access point is chosen based on features of the work, author and conceptual content. It is never discretional and takes into account conventions (though occasionally conflicting) in literary history and in the other sources of information, such as directories (Dunsire, 2020).

Access point, authorised access point and variant access point are formulations specified by ICP. The principles intentionally avoided the use of the term 'heading', a term now deemed obsolete, dating back to the catalogue cards. ICP states:

- an *access point* is a name, term, code, etc., representing a specific entity
- an *authorised access point* is a standardised access point representing an entity
- a *variant access point* is an alternative to an authorised access point representing an entity.

In many databases, an access point can potentially be any data linked to a resource; the data can be combined with any other data, including data inferred from the abstract. The access point enables the catalogue to answer specific questions:

- which works by an author
- which expressions of a work
- which manifestations of a work
- which items of a work
- which works about a subject
- which works pertaining to a class

are owned by the library or, more precisely, have been described in the catalogue by the library? In formulating it, consideration is given both to data as they appear on the source (e.g. on the title page), data that perhaps have been normalised in the access point (e.g. the name 'Leonardo da Vinci' normalised to 'Leonardo, da Vinci, 1452–1519') and to information derived from literary criticism and directories.

The access point is a structured description, based on a form of the name of the entity, to which can be added values expressing other attributes of the entity, e.g. the dates of birth and death for the *entity agent*. The form by which the entity name and title are commonly known is adopted, which may differ from the form that appears on the described resource.

This concerns, therefore, the *principle of common use* (already present in Cutter's *Rules*), according to which the form used in the creation of the access point for the creator and the title coincides with that used by the majority of the users of a community. The two criteria – original form (or form on the resource) and conventional form (or form used in the catalogue) – can conflict. Moreover, the form of the author's name and of the title to be used for the access point is not absolute; it is delimited to a linguistic and cultural area. It raises the troubling question of the language of the catalogue, never clarified, not even by ICP, to be solved in the future, apparently, in a pragmatic way, with the help of technology that could convert the various forms according to the language preferred by the reader. For example, which title should be chosen for the famous collection of oriental tales *One Thousand and One Nights*: the title in English? In Arabic the title is: ألف ليلة وليلة. And in Persian the title is: هزار و يک ش

In brief, the process of constructing an access point involves three stages:

1 find name and title used to represent each entity
2 select a form of name and title
3 add qualifiers as needed to distinguish among similar names or titles.

Its formulation implies, thus, three actions: the *choice* and the decision regarding the *form* of the name or the title being controlled. By *form* is meant both the language and script (including the linguistic variants) in which to formulate the name or title; furthermore, the order of citation of the elements of the name or title. Some examples are: William Shakespeare or Shakespeare, William; Dante Alighieri or Alighieri, Dante; George Orwell or Orwell, George or his real name Eric Arthur Blair; William Turner or Turner, William or Joseph Mallord William Turner; Alice Monroe Foster or Mary Alice Monroe; Leonardo da Vinci or Léonard de Vinci; Confucio, Confucius or (周) 孔丘 ; Ἀριστοτέλης, Aristotĕles or Aristotele.

The chosen name and title and their normalisation depend on the reference norms, which depend in their turn on cultural traditions, citation practices of information retrieval sources (such as encyclopedias, dictionaries and directories) and above all on readers' expectations. The latter factor may justify the differentiated display of the form of the name and title, depending on the user querying the catalogue (e.g. erudite form: Ἀριστοτέλης or Aristotĕles; common form: Aristotle). If the catalogue or search tool is sophisticated enough, the decision on which language or script to display may be an option for the user of the tool, as long as the cataloguer has properly provided the various forms and the search tool has that capability.

Qualifiers such as the date of birth and the date of death, e.g. 'Ernest Hemingway, 1899–1961', could accompany the chosen name.

The access point is a device used to collocate bibliographic descriptions related to the name or title of the access point. It provides a pointer to the related described entities in order to retrieve their bibliographic descriptions. Although one form of name or title may be given preferential status for display purposes depending on the system, one form of name or title should be as good as another to provide access to related bibliographic descriptions. It enables the establishment of a structure of relationships with the related works.

Relationships are a very important part of metadata creation. They connect entities and make the connections explicit among them. Creating relationships assists users in finding and discovering the resources they want. It is possible to establish a wide range of relationships:

- between works and their creators (for example, between novelists, poets, musicians, cartographers, designers, research institutes, orchestras, government bodies, etc. and the works they create)
- and those between: different works; the various expressions of a work; persons; corporate bodies; families; a person or a corporate body or a family and a place; a family and an unpublished resource; a corporate body and related persons etc.

Hence, the access point, on the one hand, enables the retrieval of records, while on the other hand, it enables their organisation through a *clustering* or *collocation* function. The relationships, the links, allow a user to *navigate among the entities*, among data of different types and origins, etc. In some systems, this is accomplished through the use of identifiers for the controlled names or titles controlled, as already occurs when using some data models (e.g. BIBFRAME, as we will see later).

5.2 Relationships
The FRBR and IFLA LRM conceptual models only define generic relationships. They let implementations develop other relationships, according to specific needs. IFLA LRM lists the relationships divided into *basic, responsibility, subject* and *appellation relationships*, as shown in Figure 5.1 opposite.

According to IFLA LRM, they all constitute a refinement of the apex-level relationship res 'is associated with' res. The basic relationships are those developed between the entities work, expression, manifestation and item. Responsibility relationships are established between works, expressions, manifestations and items and the agents. Agents have relationships because they are responsible for creation of the entities, or for their production or distribution or because they are their owners or custodians. Subject relationships link works to the res that represent their subject. Each res (and, thus, by extension any other entity) can be the subject of a work. Finally, naming relationships are used to link a res to its nomen. Each res can be known by one or more nomen, each of which is the denomination of a single res.

IFLA LRM presents general and abstract relationships allowing model implementers to include additional details in a uniform and consistent manner by introducing further refinements. The version of RDA, *Resource Description and Access*, published in December 2020, for instance,

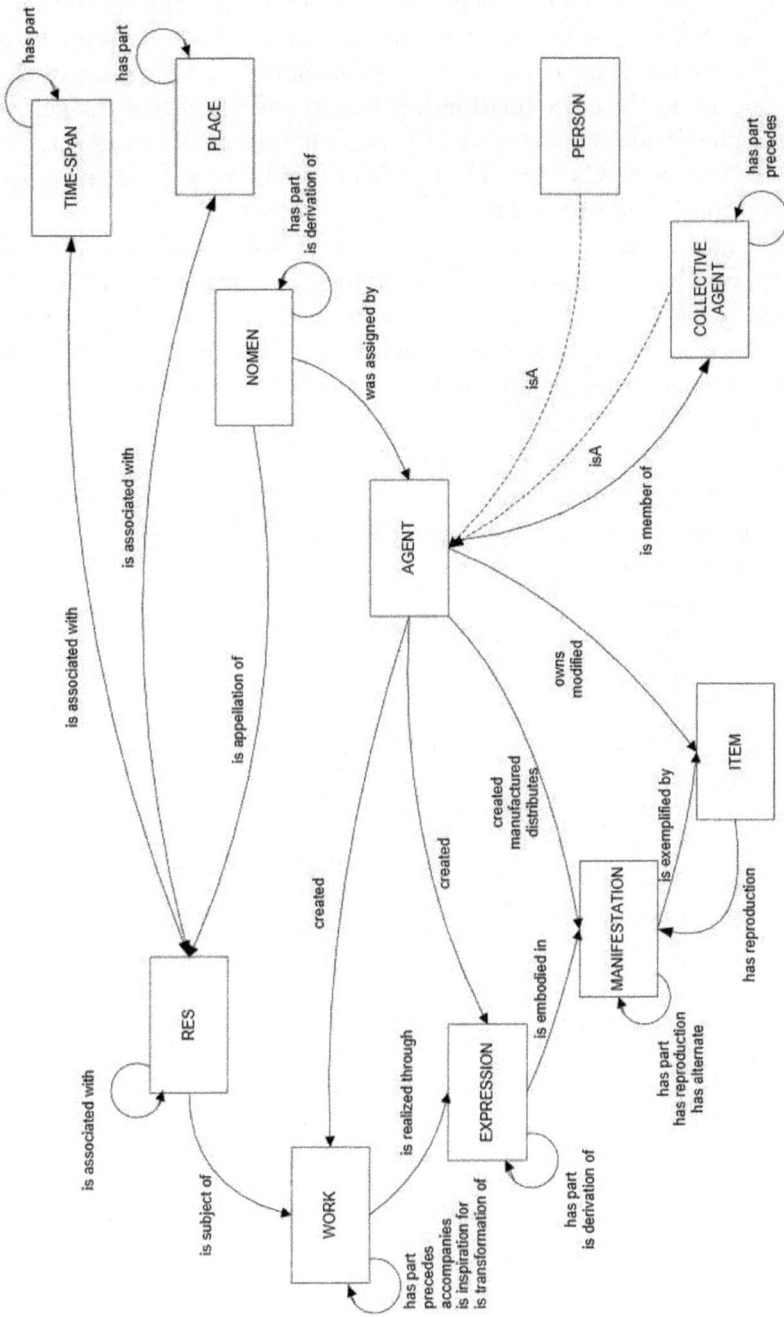

Figure 5.1 *Overview of relationships* (IFLA LRM, 2017, 86)

considerably broadens the relationships provided for by IFLA LRM and the first edition of the guidelines, which were based on FRBR. The relationship designators, that is, the terms that explain and clarify the nature of a relationship, are no longer relegated to the Appendices as they were in the first edition of RDA; each relationship has its own dedicated page; in addition, each relationship appears on the pages of the entities with which it is associated and in the Glossary. The number of relationship designators has grown enormously and this was mainly due to two factors.

First, the introduction of new entities in IFLA LRM and RDA has turned many attributes into relationships. For example, the *title proper* is no longer an attribute of the manifestation but it is expressed as a relationship between the manifestation entity and the nomen entity. This is clear from the explanatory box on the page of the RDA Toolkit dedicated to the title proper element (Figure 5.2).

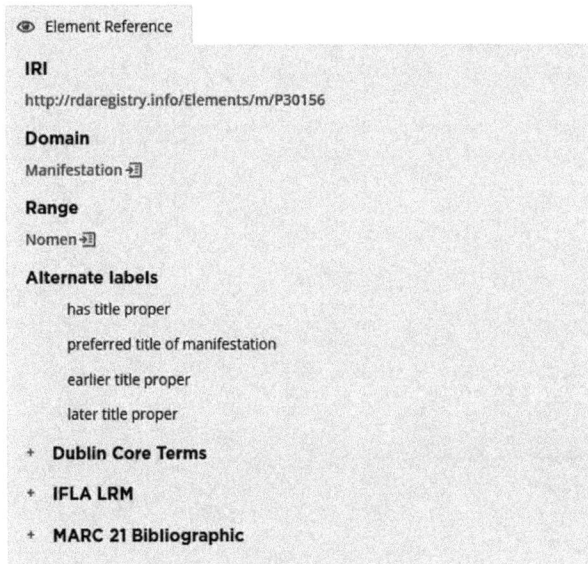

Figure 5.2 *Element reference, title proper, RDA Toolkit*

The manifestation constitutes the domain, that is, the starting point of the relationship 'has title proper' (which can be replaced by the labels 'preferred title of the manifestation', 'earlier title proper', 'later title proper') directed towards the range – a domain on an equal footing or in a co-ordinate relationship with the domain – represented by the entity nomen.

Secondly, whereas in the first edition of RDA relationship designators were defined for sets of entities considered as a whole, there are now entity-specific designators. For example, the original Toolkit devoted Appendix I to recording designators that specified the type of relationship between a FRBR/FRAD Group 2 entity and the described resource, but there was no distinction between designators depending on whether they referred to a person, a family or a corporate body. In the second edition of RDA, however, there are specific designators, so that if a person is the author of a work, the relationship designator 'person author of' will be used, whereas in the case of a family or a corporate body, 'family author of' or 'corporate body author of' will be used.

5.3 Author and title

It can be said that the Western cultural tradition for bibliographic data conventionally dates back to 1595, the year in which *The Catalogue of English Printed Books*, a commercial list of books compiled by Andrew Maunsell, was published (Maunsell, 1595). At least since that point, the author has been considered the most significant element for the identification of his or her works. This is in contrast to early Eastern cataloguing practice that preferred the title, but this practice is no longer followed.

The importance of the author has always been recognised. In today's environment of FRBR and IFLA LRM, access to the author's name is accomplished through links to the entity agent, that is, the entity responsible for creating the intellectual or artistic content of the work. An agent, according to FRBR, is a person, a family or a corporate body; according to IFLA LRM, an agent is a person or a collective agent. These two distinctions are really encompassing the same entities, just under different terminology.

An author can be a real or imagined person, an individual or a group. For example, authors include a character who existed only literarily (such as Homer), an author who hides under a pseudonym (as Elena Ferrante or Mark Twain), a stable corporate body (e.g. a municipality, a university) or a temporary corporate body (e.g. a conference, an exhibition) or a family (such as for the genealogical papers for a family).

The concept of author from a bibliographical point of view is extremely broad. It is a label that can be used as an effective tool for retrieving records: of his or her works; of works attributed to him or her; of apocryphal works attributed to him or her; of collections of images of his or her works (e.g. reproductions of Michelangelo's drawings, of Niccolò Pisano's sculptures, of Pier Luigi Nervi's buildings); even occasional resources, such as correspondence for which he or she is the only or the main creator.

The author has the responsibility for the intellectual or artistic content; this is an important criterion for the choice of the access point; it is a significant criterion, but it is not the only one.

The title may be considered the most relevant and precise element for identification of a work, because it allows the work to be named and cited. Nevertheless, it can be subject to ambiguous readings. Different resources may have the same title. Conversely, the same work may have variant titles (e.g. *One Thousand and One Nights* or *The Arabian Nights*), not to mention the target titles of translated works: Erasmus's famous *Stultitiae Laus* or *Moriae Encomium*, is translated into Dutch as *Lof der zotheid* and into English as *In Praise of Folly* or *The Praise of Folly*. Sometimes it may be difficult to determine whether these are different works or translations of the same work.

There may be translations of works, so the titles in the various languages will likely vary. The titles of films in dubbed versions in other languages are emblematic, since they are often completely different from the original title. Two examples, among many, are the film *Houseboat*, directed by Melville Shavelson, starring Cary Grant and Sofia Loren, translated into Italian as *Un Marito per Cinzia* (*A Husband for Cinzia*); and the film *Royal Wedding*, starring Fred Astaire, translated into Italian as *Sua Altezza Si Sposa* (*Her Majesty is Getting Married*). The same applies to translations of essays, particularly in the humanities and social sciences and to fiction.

It means that the title by itself, in the majority of cases, is insufficient. It is necessary to associate it with other attributes, especially the name of the author. The work/author relation is evident when a work has been written by a single author; however, the relation can be ambiguous in the case of an annotated work: is the focus on the text, i.e. the author of the target text, or on the commentary about that text, i.e. the literary critic? The ambiguity can also appear with cases of collaborative works or works of uncertain authorship.

There are very strong, well-known titles that constitute the most reliable element for finding some works. Indeed, who could search for the fable *The Sword in the Stone*, published in 1938, through the name of its author (Terence Hanbury White), famous, yet unknown to most?

There are situations in which there is no correspondence between what is declared by the source and the 'true' literary responsibility. We have previously examined the case of Giacomo Leopardi, who appeared incorrectly as the translator rather than the author of *Hymn to Neptune*. There are works considered to be original for centuries, actually written by others; e.g. Leonardo da Vinci's *Trattato della Pittura* (*Treatise on Painting*), first printed in Paris in 1651, is an abbreviated version of the *Libro di Pittura* (*Book of Painting*) compiled by his last pupil, Francesco Melzi, datable to around 1540, as was determined after the 19th-century rediscovery of the manuscript Vaticano Urbinate 1270. Some works are attributed to more than one author: *Rhetorica ad Herennium*, for example, is considered by some to be by Cicero and by others to be by Quintus Cornificius. In this situation, a relationship should be created between the work and the two presumed authors, while not attributing any intellectual responsibility to them. All these cases need an explanatory note for the user of the bibliographic data.

The act of choosing an access point is not attributing intellectual authorship, which is a task for philologists, historians and literary critics. The librarian's work is both to consider the studies carried out and to be able to conduct in-depth investigations by consulting all possible sources, other library catalogues that may have already catalogued the resource; he/she can adopt, if necessary and possible, bibliographic solutions different from those of the directories. Among other things, directories do not always propose the same solutions. It may involve contacts with publishers, to obtain direct information about the authors and their works. On the other hand, when the cataloguers opt to use a relationship designator, they assume the responsibility for attributing a specific role to an agent (e.g. a person) with respect to a work, hopefully after appropriate research and verification. The cataloguer, therefore, plays a crucial role in the making of authority files.

In conclusion, the author/title access point is the element constantly or predominantly associated with the entity work and by which it is usually cited.

5.4 Authority control: authorised access point

Authority control (or, more specifically, authority work) is the process that brings together in authority records all the forms of names for agents, works, places, and subjects used in a catalogue or database. These names are access points to reach bibliographic records and other authority records. Relationships with other access points allow navigating the metadata of different entities and discovering associations between them.

Authority control supports the catalogue's tasks to help users find, identify, select, obtain and navigate information, as stated in the International Cataloging Principles (ICP). It also ensures the *clustering function*, that is, bringing together the bibliographic records and authority records associated with an access point. To enable this clustering, authority work involves creating authority records that include the data necessary to identify an entity. Authority records then include all the forms of a name and relevant identifying information for entities found in a given catalogue or database.

The process of authority control can be provided for almost any entity:

1 agents: persons, publishers, printers, corporate bodies (including temporary ones, such as conventions and exhibitions), government bodies and officials

2 places
3 works, including titles of series
4 subjects.

There can be many forms of name for entities: an 'original' form of the name found on the first work of that entity, the form in the language and script of the author's home country, forms in various languages and scripts, etc. For example, in the case of the Japanese director and writer Akira Kurosawa, the form of name can be presented in the 'original' Japanese 黒澤 明 (and also 黒沢 明) or the form that is known in English or Spanish or some other language or script (Tillett, 1989a; Taylor and Tillett, 2004). Some of the forms of name can be considered 'authorised' by a bibliographic agency and others considered 'variant forms' of that name.

It should be noted that there is no absolute preferred form of the name, applicable to all contexts. The choice of the form is justified by its value within a linguistic and cultural context (Leonardo da Vinci or Léonard de Vinci?), by the audience to which the catalogue is addressed (Virgil or Publius Vergilius Maro) and by the norms employed. Naturally, the choice can never be arbitrary but must result from a cataloguing policy that guarantees the construction of coherent and culturally based catalogues.

Declaring one of the forms of name as the authorised access point for that entity simplifies systems, but may prove unnecessary with future software. Having a single preferred form of name was a requirement of old cataloguing rules and early software to ensure the location of the bibliographic records related to an entity. Early systems were not yet sophisticated enough to enable a user of software to prefer one form over another to suit user needs. Some still are not. However, now the various forms of names for entities can be recorded in software and used to display either a single form of name preferred by the library (its authorised access point for that entity) or a form preferred by the user. By recording in an authority record all the various forms of name, that information can be used by software to bring together the associated bibliographic records; this is the function of clustering.

Authority records can be said to define a relationship with the described resource. They can help achieve the traditional goals of the catalogue, as recalled by the Paris Principles – which works of an author and which editions of a work the library holds – and to avoid the situations of 'false attributions' or uncertain attributions which we have mentioned earlier.

The construction of authorised access should trigger a virtuous cycle for the creation of quality data. The quality of access points is determined by the authoritativeness of who establishes the relationships, the individual links (Danskin, 2013).

The concept of authority control has changed radically over the last two decades, gaining more and more prominence in catalogue management. In the microcosm of metadata, the transformation has been complete; now we are witnessing the management of granular bibliographic data, as required by the Semantic Web. The initiatives of aggregation and exchange of data at a global level (such as VIAF) and not only of bibliographic data (such as *Wikidata*) are important.[26]

5.5 Entity identifiers

As we have seen, the name of an entity can be known in different languages and scripts. The set of these different forms is associated with an identifier that becomes the *identifier for the entity* within the same dataset. The machine uses that identifier to reach the description of the resource; this allows the reader to use, during the search, one of the variant forms belonging to the same cluster.

Identifiers have appeared in publishing since the 1970s, when the International Standard Book Number (ISBN) and the International Standard Serial Number (ISSN) were introduced to identify monographs and periodicals. These were followed by the publication of the International Standard Recording Code (ISRC) and the International Standard Music Number (ISMN), aimed at other types of publishing products.

From the 1990s onwards, identifiers for intellectual works regardless of the form of presentation were developed, such as the International Standard Musical Work Code (ISWC) and the International Standard Text Code (ISTC). Their publication testifies to the increased focus on artistic and intellectual content in addition to the physical form of the described resources and it appears perfectly in line with the reflection on bibliographic description developed in those years that led to the publication of FRBR. Within FRBR specific attention was paid to the entities Work and Expression in addition to Manifestation and Item, which had already enjoyed greater consideration for some time.

From the end of the 20th century, it became necessary to identify digital resources with their metadata. This led to the birth of identifiers such as the National Bibliography Number (NBN), used exclusively by national libraries for the identification of digital resources to which no other identifiers have been assigned. Other identifiers followed, such as the Archival Resource Key (ARK) for the identification of different types of archived digital products and the Digital Object Identifier (DOI) for the identification of articles and books.

DOIs were initially used only for the identification of articles in digital journals; now DOIs are also attributed to books and parts thereof (such as chapters) and other types of resources: audio, video, software, etc. A DOI consists of a unique string of alphanumeric characters, composed of a prefix and suffix. Each DOI is associated with a set of metadata, which includes the location of the digital resource and is based on the ONline Information eXchange (ONIX) format. Since 2018, DOIs have been used by some major international commercial and scientific publishers, including Cambridge University Press, Brill, Taylor & Francis, and in Italy they have been adopted by Firenze University Press since 2020; they are based on the services offered by Crossref, an agency for DOI attribution.

Finally, alongside identifiers for resources, identifiers have been developed to identify identities used by some services – such the Virtual International Authority File Identifier (VIAF ID), the International Standard Name Identifier (ISNI) and the Open Researcher and Contributor ID (ORCID).

Libraries have been aware of the importance of identifiers since their initial appearance. They play a fundamental role in the data quality control processes. Furthermore, following the Universal Bibliographic Control (UBC) Project, it became evident that national bibliographic agencies cannot adopt a common form of access point for the same entity (given difference in languages, local cultural preferences, etc.). However, the goal of international sharing of authority data and UBC can be still pursued by connecting the variant forms in an international virtual authority file; variant forms can be associated with a unique identifier, allowing sharing of authority data from different sources and displaying the reader's preferred form.

As it will be described further below, VIAF and ISNI are part of broader projects of international co-operation and authority control; both represent two of the most remarkable initiatives facing the challenge of identifying in a reliable way agents, geographic names, etc. and the works associated with them in the network of global recorded knowledge. Their philosophy is inspired by the UBC's humanistic ideal of sharing collective knowledge, promoting cultural diversity and simplifying the work of bibliographic agencies and libraries, many of which participate in both systems. The quality of the source data is crucial: the more accurate the data, the greater the benefits that VIAF and ISNI can bring to the library, archival and museum communities by aggregating and connecting data.

Interoperability between identifiers is of strategic value in placing bibliographic and authority data at the centre of a solid network of identity information and connecting them with other datasets than those developed by libraries (Žumer, 2009).

To make this possible, however, it is necessary that the identifiers are constructed in compliance with certain principles, such as uniqueness and permanence. Uniqueness ensures that each identifier is associated with only one entity and that there is absolute correspondence between the entity and the identifier within a given domain. Permanence guarantees the stability of an identifier over time and it is ensured when the identifier is based on shared and transparent governance. In addition to these requirements, actionability and persistence have particular relevance for identifiers associated with digital resources. Actionability consists of the possibility of being referred directly from an identifier to a resource or to the set of metadata with which it is associated. Persistence guarantees the retrieval of digital objects over a long period of time and can be ensured through the processing of stable codes, uniquely and permanently associated with entities or parts of them.

5.6 VIAF

VIAF, the Virtual International Authority File,[27] launched on 6 August 2003 by the Library of Congress, Deutsche Nationalbibliothek and Bibliothèque nationale de France, with Online Computer Library Center (OCLC) operating it, currently holds data produced by over 40 organisations in some 30 countries around the world. Its aim is the automatic connection, through the development of matching algorithms, of the authority records produced by the participating national agencies, making them available on the web through a global and free authority service. VIAF, using a single interface, enables the virtual query of authority records in the language and script used by the end-user. The variant forms of a name (linguistic, graphic, in the order of the elements) can co-exist within the same record without any conflict, since none of them is declared to be absolute. It guarantees respect for the linguistic diversity of each country and each bibliographic agency; libraries and bibliographic agencies can choose the preferred form of a name according to their own language and script and, most importantly, according to their own cultural tradition.

Consider, for example, a query of the name Herman Melville. The person is associated with the *VIAF identifier* (VIAF ID) to which are linked various forms of the name:

VIAF ID: 27068555 (Personal)
Permalink: http://viaf.org/viaf/27068555
Melville, Herman, 1819–1891
Melville, Herman
Herman Melville
זמרה, ליוולמ‎, 1819–1891
Мелвилл, Г. Герман 1819–1891
نامره ،لفلم‎ 1819–1891
...

VIAF began with authority records for personal names, and it now also contains authority records for geographical names, names of organisations, works and expressions. The widening of the area of interest can be correlated to the so-called *FRBRisation* process that has affected catalogues. The original authority data, enriched and made reliable by the interconnection between different communities, evolve from simple access points for bibliographic descriptions to stable data with identifiers that offer endless possibilities of reuse in the Semantic Web.

The sharing of authority data results in the strengthening of data through the comparison, the simplification of authority control at the international level, the reduction of cataloguing costs (thanks to a distributed working practice) and the availability of authority data in different languages and scripts. As noted above, end-users (mainly librarians) can reuse VIAF data free of charge, thanks to an open licence. Data are presented in a number of *output* formats that can be used and accessed both inside and outside the library community. VIAF, as a tool of the library community, offers new exposure to the data of each of its international members and contributors. That is particularly important for evaluating data based on its provenance, highlighting and improving the domains of expertise of each project participant. Libraries and cultural institutions have unique knowledge of the identities related to the specialised collections they manage, with specialists who have excellent knowledge of their domain identities. This is why the responsibility for authority data is not and should not be concentrated exclusively in the hands of national libraries.

VIAF includes many variant forms, but what is relevant for the machine, for the catalogue management software, is the VIAF ID, the identifier to which all forms of the name are linked. In a contemporary perspective of authority control, the whole cluster is subject to control, in other words, all are variant forms of the name. For monitor display in a specific environment, a form of the name, the *preferred form* for that environment, is chosen from all the variants by which an entity is known. It is the authorised (that is, authority-controlled) access point within a linguistic and cultural context. The form of the name, therefore, may vary between a catalogue intended for Japanese readers and a catalogue intended for Russian, Chinese, Croatian or Italian readers. The identifiers, therefore, serve to 'make the machine understand' that Leonardo, da Vinci, 1452–1519 is the same person entity that in VIAF is qualified as VIAF ID: 24604287 (Personal). The VIAF identifier follows the structure:

VIAF ID: 24604287 (Personal).
Permalink: http://viaf.org/viaf/24604287.

The Permalink, or *permanent link*, is a type of URL that refers, in this case, to the entity person Leonardo da Vinci, 1452–1519. Dates of birth and death are qualifiers and form part of the access point.

5.7 ISNI

The International Standard Name Identifier (ISNI)[28] is an ISO standard (ISO 27729), published in March 2012. It is a way to identify the *public identity* of people and organisations uniquely. It creates permanent numeric identifiers (in batch mode and on request) for the names of entities associated with content creation, including authors, composers, publishers, printers, researchers, inventors, artists, musicians, actors and others. In today's environment, ISNI is an effective tool for facilitating the disambiguation of homonyms, name variants, and the attribution of works to their respective authors within databases across the publishing production chain. The standard defines three entities:

- *part*: a real entity, i.e. person, organisation, fictitious character
- *public identity*: the name by which a *part* is known
- *name*.

Each public identity is associated with an ISNI number. A *part* can have multiple names and multiple forms of the name, alternative spellings and scripts, linguistic variants and variants due to transliterations. For example, a search for Thomas Stearns Eliot produces the following result consisting of the *ISNI identifier* associated with the person and the variant forms of the name:

ISNI 0000 0001 2133 9888
Eliot (T. S.)
Eliot (T.S.; 1888–1965)
Eliot, T. S. (British poet, 1888–1965)
Eliot, T. S. (former owner)
Eliot, T. S. (Thomas Stearns)
Eliot, Th. S.
Eliot, Thomas S.
Eliot, Thomas Stearn
Eliot, Thomas Stearnes
Eliot (Thomas Stearns)
...

The ISNI identifier is composed of 16 characters, the last of which is a control character (a decimal digit or the character 'X'). It has all the required features for an identifier on the web. That is, it is unique, persistent and reusable. The assignment of an ISNI is based on metadata provided to the system by the different contributors, namely, copyright management companies, libraries, publishers and distributors.

ISNI is designed as a 'bridge' identifier to enable various partners to exchange information about an entity without revealing confidential information. Indeed, it keeps only the minimum set of metadata required to differentiate and disambiguate public entities. Links between parts' public identities are established only if the relationship is intentional. Otherwise, they are not created, to ensure privacy. Other information remains in the database protected by conditional access.

ISNI has refined its matching algorithms to make entity identification more reliable. Each ISNI identifier is assigned to a public identity only when at least three titles of works are associated with the person. From the outset, the system attributes different weights (scores) to the data providers, based on their provenance and the degree of probability of them being in direct contact with the entity to be identified. The highest level of reliance is given to contributors who obtain data directly from the person or organisation close to the identity. ISNI is independent of language, domain and geographic territory. It is interoperable, in the sense that a fundamental part of its function is to map other identifiers, standard or proprietary (Armitage et al., 2020).

6

Exchange Formats and Descriptive Standards: MARC and ISBD

As Michael Gorman stated on many occasions (Gorman, 2003), MARC and ISBD are two sides of the same coin: the first technological, the second bibliographic. MARC was designed in the early 1960s by the Library of Congress and ISBD was conceived in the late 1960s in the context of IFLA (Guerrini and Possemato, 2015). Let's look at each.

6.1 MARC, UNIMARC, MARC21

MARC is a machine-readable format for recording and exchanging bibliographic data. In the early 1960s, the Library of Congress decided to convert its card catalogues into electronic catalogues, introducing the possibility of disseminating data also in digital format. In 1964 a team co-ordinated by Henriette Avram was asked to create a draft of a machine-readable record. This initiative led to the MARC Pilot Project, which involved 16 libraries of various kinds that worked on the creation and distribution of digital bibliographic data and the evaluation of the possible uses of the data produced by the Library of Congress (Library of Congress, Information Systems Office, 1968). The experimentation resulted in a format, called MARC I, which contained, in a nutshell, some characteristics of the current one. The work proceeded in collaboration with the British Library and in 1968 the MARC II format was presented and used as a model for subsequent formats.

In the 1970s MARC spread rapidly with the diffusion of automation in libraries. The USA tried to standardise the various formats by creating the USMARC Format for Bibliographic Data; however, several national and international variants emerged (e.g. INTERMARC in France and Belgium, later replaced by UNIMARC in France; CANMARC in Canada; UKMARC in England; ANNAMARC in Italy; RUSMARC in Russia). In 1999 MARC21 was published as a result of the collaboration between the Library of Congress, the British Library and the National Library of Canada to adopt a single format for the whole Anglo-American world. MARC21 is maintained by the Library of Congress.

MARC is very significant, because it is still able to manage highly formalised data and is used by the majority of libraries around the world.

In 1973 the general structure for transmitting MARC became the international standard ISO 2709. A record that conforms to ISO 2709 consists of three parts:

1 the first part is called the *leader*, which contains in encoded form general data for the processing of the record
2 the second part is called the *directory*, which presents the index of all the fields contained
3 the third part hosts all the *fields* that are part of a record.

A MARC record's structure consists of *fields*, *subfields*, *tags* and *indicators*.

Fields are where specific data are recorded, such as the title, the statement of responsibility and the subject string provided as access for the bibliographic description. Each field can be divided into subfields that contain specific parts of the field, for example, title proper, other title information (remainder of title) and statement of responsibility. Each field is associated with a three-character string called a *tag* that identifies it. An example of a tag is '245', which in MARC21 format marks the data related to the title and intellectual responsibility of the resource. The tag is followed by two elements called indicators, which value, interpret and integrate the data entered in the field. One example is the second indicator of the tag '245', which indicates the number of characters to be omitted when filing a title that begins with an initial article or other non-filing characters.

Some MARC tags are correlated with the type of data to be recorded in the fields they designate. MARC21 organises the fields by type, using the first character of each tag:

0XX	Control information, numbers and codes
1XX	Main entry
2XX	Titles and title paragraph (title, edition, imprint)
3XX	Physical description, etc.
4XX	Series statements
5XX	Notes
6XX	Subject access fields
7XX	Added entries other than subject or series; linking fields
8XX	Series added entries; location and alternate graphics
9XX	Reserved for local implementation (can be used to add other types of information to records) (Avram, 1975).

All subfields are indicated in coded form by two characters: a lowercase letter or a number, preceded by a delimiter, for example $a. The delimiter is actually the decimal character 31 of the ISO 646 standard, but is displayed in different ways by programs that use MARC ($, |, etc.). It is worth noting that MARC is a format of exchange between computers and that MARC records presented by bibliographic management software (both in the input and the display stage) are intended for the understanding of the information by a human being. No one would be able to work readily on a record in native ISO 2709 format.

UNIversal MAchine Readable Cataloguing (UNIMARC) is a MARC format proposed by IFLA in 1977. UNIMARC was originally intended as an intermediate format between different national MARCs. According to this vision, a national bibliographic agency, in order to exchange records with other agencies, would need only two programs: an export program in UNIMARC format and an import program from UNIMARC format. UNIMARC was used (and is still used) as a native MARC format in many countries.

UNIMARC appeared, at the time of its release, as an innovative format in at least three aspects. The first is the functional organisation of the fields within the record (functional blocks of tags). For example, in UNIMARC all accesses related to intellectual responsibility are grouped in tags with '7' as the first number. The second concerns the provision of a functional tag block for links between different records (the 4XX block). Finally, the third concerns the one-to-one alignment between the granularity expected by ISBD and the fields (ISBD areas) and subfields (ISBD elements) of the UNIMARC functional block for description (2XX). A UNIMARC record does not ever include ISBD punctuation, since conventional punctuation can be created by UNIMARC coding. This is in contrast to MARC21, which includes both the field and subfield tags as well as the necessary punctuation.

In addition to bibliographic record formats, UNIMARC and MARC21 allow the creation of exchange records also for information under authority control (UNIMARC Authorities; MARC 21 Authorities) and for information related to library holdings (UNIMARC Holdings; MARC 21 Holdings).

The standardised structure of information is provided by the ISO standard governing MARC and UNIMARC, ISO 2709. This structure is based on *labels*, *directories* and *data fields* and is still employed by some systems even today. However, after the emergence of the XML markup language, MARC records can also be exchanged using XML syntax. There is dedicated software that allows the automatic conversion of existing records from MARC21 into MARCXML. Also, the ISO 25577 standard of 2008 established the rules for the creation of a MARC record that with equal granularity and semantics adopts a recording and presentation of data with XML markup instead of the ISO 2709 markup.

In 2002, an article entitled 'MARC Must Die' appeared in *Library Journal*, in the Digital Libraries column by Roy Tennant, characterising MARC as an anachronistic format because of its rigidity and lack of granularity. The title was ironically viewed by the MARC maintainers as an auspicious sign, given that it is still 'alive and well,' Even Tennant himself acknowledged elsewhere:

> . . . although with the awareness of its transition to something more functional. MARC has been able to accommodate and convey structured bibliographic information, providing a mode of exchange in the library community (less in other domains, such as archives) for over half a century. Its longevity is a commendable achievement for a format designed for the recording and exchange of bibliographic data in a context completely different from the present one.
>
> (Tennant, 2002; 2017).

Bibliographic data are still bound to the unitary *record-oriented* structure imposed by MARC, and changing to a new *entity-oriented* approach would be very difficult to implement. This would require not only the conversion of millions of records worldwide,[29] but the configuration of new management systems, new exchange methodologies and, above all, new approaches to information management, with considerable investments in terms of technological infrastructure.

MARC's usefulness has been welcomed by libraries, especially by providers of cataloguing systems, paving the way for a series of collaborative and exchange activities, the first of which is copy cataloguing (carried out at different service levels), with the aim of avoiding, if possible, the cataloguing of each resource from scratch.

The introduction of MARC, in its various formulations, has required and imposed, over the years, an enormous investment both in terms of adaptation of systems and training of librarians. This general mobilisation has ensured the longevity of the format, although it has generated some important misunderstandings, such as 'cataloguing in MARC' instead of cataloguing according to the rules (AACR2, etc.) and then structuring the information in MARC for the purpose of exchange with other institutions.

The longevity of MARC and of some of its specific varieties (first MARC 21 and, hence, UNIMARC) has been fostered by the activity of a large community, which has overseen its constant evolution into a hyper-specialised and hyper-detailed data structuring format.

BIBFRAME has the ambition to replace MARC, but it doesn't have, at the moment, the same degree of maturity. Therefore, MARC has to continue in its role and function. The Library of Congress, for example, still invests in its periodic updates in parallel with the investments required for the growth and dissemination of BIBFRAME.

6.2 BIBFRAME

Millions of records are structured in MARC21 and, to a much lesser extent, in UNIMARC. For over 20 years, however, a gap has been perceived between the data produced by the institutions of recorded memory and the techniques for the implementation of the Semantic Web and the need for technological adaptation has emerged. As they are structured, records have proved to be inadequate for the web. Furthermore, MARC is used only within the library community, making the exchange with external communities, such as archives and museums, impossible. Data sharing (*interoperability*) is one of the requirements of the Semantic Web.

To begin a radical transformation in the library environment, the Library of Congress published *On the Record* in 2008, thus marking the transition to the Bibliographic Framework Transition Initiative. The publication recommends joint work with the communities interested in developing a supporting framework for bibliographic data.

In 2010, OCLC published another important document 'Best Practices for Creating Sharable Metadata' (last updated 16 August 2022), in which it attempted to determine the most frequently used MARC fields to reuse them in future metadata schemes.

Then in 2011 a substantial initiative to replace MARC with a more appropriate format for the Semantic Web was announced: the Bibliographic Framework Initiative. This initiative aims to enable the reuse of the millions of MARC records generated by libraries in the context of the Semantic Web, facilitating the assembly of data in new and more granular architectures. *Bibliographic Framework as a web of data: linked data model and supporting services* (BIBFRAME), issued by the Library of Congress on 21 November 2012, was the outcome of a process of discussion on new types of resources, on the functions of the catalogue, on the relevance of MARC and on cataloguing standards. It was the first step of a road map that will lead to the proposal of a new environment for libraries, a new bibliographic ecosystem. It can be defined both as a *data model* and as an *ontology*; it aims towards:

1 a greater level of data identification and analysis
2 a greater attention to controlled vocabularies

3 a greater use of terms compared to current cataloguing codes
4 an emphasis on relationships
5 greater flexibility and greater use of controlled entries
6 the conversion of bibliographic data into linked data, seen as:
    6.1   an evolution and not revolution
    6.2   a basis for starting a comparison and discussion within the library
        community
7 the use of the web as a model for expressing and connecting data
8 the use of URIs, an effective tool for identifying entities, attributes and
   relationships
9 its adoption beyond the library community.

BIBFRAME defines a general guideline, encompassing:

1 the expectation that next-generation integrated library systems will be
   oriented toward a resource-based architecture, in which the object of
   cataloguing will be an individual item, a data element and not the entire
   record
2 the possibility for each resource to be linked to other resources
3 the opportunity for the cataloguer to obtain and reuse data from the
   web, thus avoiding the need to create new objects
4 the use of controlled terms and access to lists of terms and vocabularies
   available on the web; for example Open Metadata Registry and
   ID.LOC.GOV – Linked Data Service
5 the possibility of defining, at the system configuration level, the creation
   of URIs, thus ensuring that each new resource will be automatically
   enriched by a URI
6 the shift from the traditional cataloguing environment to a new system
   consisting of linked data (which involves the Library of Congress,
   national libraries of many countries, bibliographic agencies) and requires
   in-depth reflection by everyone who creates and disseminates
   bibliographic data.[30]

The BIBFRAME data model is continuously updated in respect of classes
and properties, especially regarding the conversion from MARC 21.[31] The
first version of BIBFRAME, called 1.0, was followed in 2016 by version 2.0,
which, as Figure 6.1 opposite shows, identifies three main classes that can
be subdivided in subclasses:

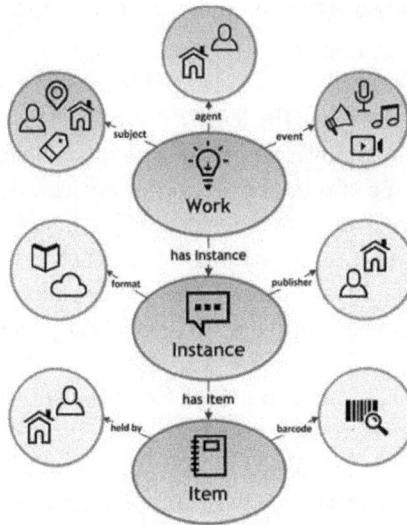

Figure 6.1 *BIBFRAME data model*

- *Work*: the highest level of abstraction. A work reflects the conceptual essence of the catalogued resource: authors, languages and what it is about (subjects).
- *Instance*: the material embodiment of a work, for example, a particular published form. An *Instance* may reflect information such as its publisher, place and date of publication and format.
- *Item*: a copy, physical or electronic, of an instance, expressing information such as location and inventory number.

In addition, BIBFRAME further defines some key concepts that have relationships to the core classes, such as:

- *Agent*: Agents are people, organisations, jurisdictions, etc., associated with a *Work* or *Instance* through roles such as author, editor, artist, photographer, composer, illustrator.
- *Subject*: A Work might be 'about' one or more concepts defined as 'subject' of the Work. These concepts include topics, places, temporal expressions, events, works, instances, items, agents, etc.
- *Event*: occurrences, the recording of which may be the content of a Work, as with the proceedings of a conference, where the conference is the event.

Following the development of version 2.0 of BIBFRAME, an ambitious pilot project was initiated. It consisted of two phases. The first involved the conversion of MARC records into BIBFRAME, while the second involved the direct creation of data in BIBFRAME by means of a description input tool. This tool is radically innovative: moving beyond the traditional approach of the MARC record to a true construction of entities defined by means of a set of attributes and relationships, designated with terminology taken from the RDA guidelines. The integration of the RDA with the BIBFRAME ontology makes it possible to outline a new method of bibliographic data management and to develop a vision of metadata procedures centred on entity construction.

In the summer of 2022, the Library of Congress set up LC MARVA, the staff input/update interface used to create or update BIBFRAME through an intuitive interface (i.e. not an RDF view of the data). MARVA replaces the BIBFRAME Editor (BFE) that was used for some early prototypes. As of November 2021, the BIBFRAME Editor was renamed MARVA, which is Avram spelled backwards, in remembrance of Henriette Avram.

6.3 ISBD
ISBD was the first bibliographic standard shared at an international level. It has been the most influential and long-lasting model in the history of cataloguing. It aims at the identification of the essential data for description; the first step is the recognition of a logical function of the single descriptive elements; they are consistently reassembled in predetermined areas, with respect to their formulation on sources of information. Punctuation and conventional signs precede the descriptive elements in the form of an identification code. The standard has greatly promoted the harmonisation of description at an international level and has contributed to the creation of a common mindset among cataloguers (Gorman, 2014). The standard has been applied directly in countries without their own standards or with inadequate codes for description. Since the 1970s and 1980s, the national bibliographies and catalogues of nearly all libraries worldwide have been (and continue to be) compiled with the ISBD formalisation. It is only since the second decade of the 21st century that some national bibliographies and some catalogues have abandoned it in favour of other standards.

The formalisation and conventionality of description date back to the 19th-century attempts made by libraries that placed themselves at the centre of bibliographical systems that included collective cataloguing (Biagetti, 2001). They were formalised with the *Rules* by Jewett in 1853 and emphasised by the *Henkle Report* in 1946 (Library of Congress, Director of the Processing Department, 1946) and the *Rules for Descriptive Cataloging* of the Library of Congress in 1949 (Library of Congress, Descriptive Cataloging Division, 1949). They reached a completely conscious and universal formulation with the creation of ISBD in the late 1960s and early 1970s.

At the International Meeting of Cataloguing Experts (IMCE), sponsored by IFLA and held in Copenhagen in 1969, the participants decided to develop a uniform bibliographic description model. Michael Gorman, assisted by Akos Domanovszky, was asked to conduct a comparative analysis of the performance of eight of the major bibliographic agencies responsible for drafting national bibliographies and the Library of Congress (acting as the national bibliographic agency of the USA). In May 1971, a preliminary standard appeared, the SBD, *Standard Bibliographic Description (for Single Volume and Multi-Volume Monographic Publications)*, a 32–page mechanically reproduced typescript. By 1973 SBD becomes ISBD: the adjective *International* was added to the initial acronym and it became the *International Standard Bibliographic Description*. ISBD had already been taken into consideration by many cataloguing committees in drafting national description standards.

In 1974, the IFLA Committee on Cataloguing published the *First Standard Edition* of the *International Standard Bibliographic Description for Monographic Publications* ISBD(M). According to this standard, the selected elements are presented (if necessary, integrated) within a predefined conventional scheme which is divided into seven areas defined by homogeneous categories of data. The elements are recorded, preceded by, or included within punctuation, which is also conventional. The convention is referred to as *format*, a word borrowed or requalified by computer language. The normalised disposition of bibliographic information implies the analysis and conversion of data from typographic to cataloguing language.

The drafting of the standard for serials raised the need for a general scheme with reference functions. ISBD(G) was published in 1977, a manual configured as a guide to which all other standards should conform to ensure homogeneity. In 1977 several versions of ISBD were published: ISBD(S), dedicated to the description of serials, journals, newspapers, series of monographs; ISBD(CM), dedicated to cartographic material; ISBD(NBM), dedicated to the so-called 'non-book' material (sound recordings, posters, etc.). All ISBD manuals are now structured in eight areas. Compared to the first scheme, a specific area for the different types of resources was added, which was assigned as area 3, while the previous area 3 became area 4 and the numbers assigned to the other areas were adjusted accordingly. The manuals have the same numerical sequence and adopt the terminology of ISBD(G).

During the 1970s, 1980s and 1990s more ISBD manuals and guidelines appeared. In 1978 an update of ISBD(M) was published. In 1980 ISBD(A) was edited, devoted to the description of antiquarian books published before 1801 (for other standards before 1830) or of antiquarian interest, that is, produced manually or by methods that continue the tradition of manual printing; and ISBD(PM), for printed music. In 1990 ISBD(CF), *Computer Files* and *Guidelines for the Application of the ISBDs to the Description of Component Part* were released. These were recommendations (something less than a standard) formulated for the compilation of analytical records, the analytical entry for contributions published in a non-autonomous form, i.e. within a miscellaneous volume or an issue of a journal. In the original project, the recommendations should have consisted of a standard initially entitled ISBD(An), *Analysis* and subsequently ISBD(CP), *Component Parts*. After the circulation of several drafts, IFLA opted for *Guidelines*, since analysis records were considered a special procedure. In 1997 *International Standard Bibliographic Description for Electronic Resources* (ISBD(ER)) – an update of ISBD(CF) – was published. It is significant to note the modification in the title, as a consequence of new acquisitions and awareness. The term *resource* appeared to designate a specific category, namely *Electronic Resources*, that was intended to include all types of digital objects. At the beginning of the 2000s a working group was established to draft a standard for the description of manuscripts, an objective that turned out not to be feasible.

However, integration of manuscripts and other unpublished resources into the ISBD was finally accomplished in the 2011 update.

The manuals were intended to be constantly reviewed by working committees responsible for the publication of five-year updates (periodicity disregarded). In 1987 revised editions were published of ISBD(M), ISBD(CM), ISBD(NBM) and in 1988 of ISBD(S), in 1990 of ISBD(PM) and ISBD(CF) and in 1991 of ISBD(A). For ISBD(A), the reference to books published before 1801 was removed, giving evidence of manual composition priority over chronology. In 1992 the revision of ISBD(G) appeared.

In 1992, the IFLA Section on Cataloguing established the Study Group on the Functional Requirements for Bibliographic Records (FRBR). Subsequently, the ISBD Review Group suspended most of the updates. In 1998, the FRBR Study Group published the *Final Report* and the ISBD Review Group resumed work to revise the texts to ensure consistency between the prescriptions of the standard and the requirements of FRBR for basic-level national bibliographic records. ISBD(S) became *International Standard Bibliographic Description for Serials and Other Continuing Resources* (ISBD(CR)), published in 2002. Revised editions of ISBD(M) and

ISBD(G) were released respectively in 2002 and 2004. ISBD(CM) and ISBD(ER) were subjected to the international maintenance process but meanwhile the work on the consolidated edition of ISBD was taking place and their publication was suspended. IFLA published the *Preliminary Edition* of the *Consolidated ISBD* in 2007, which was a merging and updating of the standards of the ISBD family, and in 2011 the definitive *Consolidated Edition* replaced all previous single ISBDs.

6.4 ISBD: Consolidated Edition

The *Consolidated Edition* contains significant innovations compared to previous individual ISBDs, including Area 0, called Content form and media type area; Area 0 includes the elements of *content form* and *media type* for general designation of material. These elements have been introduced after a decade of discussion. The text avoids redundancies, specifies when an element is mandatory, clarifies the object of the description, pays attention to multi-part monographic resources, examines the sources of information to guarantee terminological consistency and carefully considers the characteristics of non-Roman scripts. It renames area 5 to permit a homogeneous description of all resources. It renames area 8 Resource identifier and terms of availability area (the emphasis given to the identifier is noteworthy). Finally, it includes new definitions in the glossary.

Elena Escolano Rodrìguez, chair of the ISBD Review Group for many years, recalls in the *Introduction* that the work has been guided by the following objectives and principles:

1 provide consistent stipulations for description of all types of published resources, to the extent that uniformity is possible and specific stipulations for specific types of resources as required to describe those resources
2 provide the stipulations for compatible descriptive cataloguing worldwide in order to aid the international exchange of bibliographic records between national bibliographic agencies and throughout the international library and information community (including producers and publishers)
3 define different levels of description, including those needed by national bibliographic agencies, national libraries and other libraries
4 specify the descriptive elements needed to identify and select a resource
5 remember that the focus of the description is on the set of elements of information, rather than on the display or use of those elements in a specific automated system
6 base stipulations on cost-effectiveness.[32]

6.5 ISBD: purposes

The *Introduction* of the Consolidated ISBD recalls its main purpose: to be a fundamental standard for the promotion of Universal Bibliographic Control and for making the basic bibliographic data relating to all types of resources published in any country universally and easily available in an internationally accepted form. It provides uniform criteria for sharing bibliographic information, specifies the elements that form a description, and prescribes the order in which the elements should be presented and the punctuation by which they should be identified. ISBD aims to:

1 make records from different sources interchangeable, so that records produced in one country can be easily accepted in library catalogues or other bibliographic lists in any other country
2 assist in the interpretation of records across language barriers, so that records produced for users of one language can be interpreted by users of other languages
3 assist in the conversion of bibliographic records to electronic form
4 enhance the portability of bibliographic data in the Semantic Web environment and the interoperability of the ISBD with other content standards.

ISBD implies a normalisation of the recording architecture, which is divided into a descriptive structure organised in areas, for each of which it prescribes the internal and external information sources of the resource (e.g. the container of a set of audio CDs). This clarification is one great merit of the standard. Elements derived from non-prescribed sources are enclosed in square brackets or recorded in the Note area. Ambiguous information (or information considered so) is followed by the necessary explanations; inaccuracies are indicated or corrected, when necessary, by means of conventional signs declaring the operation (e.g. square brackets for a cataloguer's personal addition). Normalised or standard descriptions do not arbitrarily reconstruct data that are absent from the resource or present but inaccurately formulated.

Consolidated ISBD has nine areas, of which it specifies the elements:

0 Content form and media type area
1 Title and statement of responsibility area
2 Edition area
3 Material or type of resource specific area
4 Publication, production, distribution, etc., area
5 Material description area

6 Series and multipart monographic resource area
7 Note area
8 Resource identifier and terms of availability area

In summary, ISBD establishes:

- the source of information for each area
- the elements to be selected
- the areas in which elements are to be recorded, and
- the order and the method in which elements are to be recorded.

Since 2016, on the instructions of IFLA's Cataloguing Section, the ISBD standard and the bibliographic models (FRBR and now IFLA LRM) fall directly under the authority of the IFLA Committee on Standards. In the same year, the ISBD Linked Data Study Group published *Guidelines for Use of ISBD as Linked Data*. These guidelines are intended for developers of applications that enable libraries to display ISBD metadata for the Semantic Web. The 2011 *Consolidated Edition* was the subject of a revision published in 2021 under the title *ISBD: International Standard Bibliographic Description. 2021 Update to the 2011 Consolidated Edition*. It has some large changes. It now includes stipulations for unpublished resources, for example, expanding cartographic materials provisions to enlarge information on celestial cartographic reources, and adding stipulations taking into consideration what the separate component parts of a publication dealt with.

The need to revise the standard had been felt for some time. Even before the publication of the 2011 *Consolidated Edition*, proposals for changes started to arrive from the ISBD user community. However, the preparation of the new text did not start immediately because the ISBD Review Group was engaged in other parallel projects. Moreover, the 2011 edition was aligned with FRBR. In 2016 the Task Group for the Analysis of the Alignment and Impact of IFLA LRM to ISBD was set up in order to see what changes would need to be made to ISBD to bring it in line with the new IFLA LRM conceptual model under development. In 2017 the mapping of ISBD and IFLA LRM was published, subsequently revised and updated in 2018. However, a study is still under way to understand the real impact this alignment may have and how it will affect the current structure of ISBD (Escolano Rodriguez, 2022).

7

RDA: Some Basics

RDA, *Resource Description and Access*, is a set of guidelines developed by the Committee of Principals for AACR, the institution that had promoted, updated and published the *Anglo-American Cataloguing Rules 2nd Edition* (AACR2). In 2004, the revision of the Anglo-American Rules began at the urging of the Joint Steering Committee for Revision of AACR; the Joint Steering Committee had already tried to assess possible developments of the model in 1997 at a meeting held in Toronto among the world's leading cataloguing experts. However, in 2005, after realising the obsolescence of AACR2, it was decided to take a completely different approach; the draft of the first part of RDA was published at the end of that year.

Over the next two years other parts of the standard were published and in 2008 the first complete draft of the new revised text was prepared, delivered in June 2009. It was published in a loose-leaf volume and in an online version called *RDA Toolkit* in June 2010. On 6 November 2015 a new structure for the governance of RDA was established: the RDA Steering Committee (RSC), born from the merger of the Joint Steering Committee for the Development of RDA (JSC) and the Committee of Principals (COP). The new organisation, responsible for RDA projects and the publication of its updates, is composed of representatives from the Library of Congress, the British Library, Library and Archives Canada, the National Library of Australia, the Chartered Institute of Library and Information Professionals and the Deutsche Nationalbibliothek.

Since 31 March 2013 RDA has been adopted by the Library of Congress and many other American, Australian and European libraries. There have also been different translations of the standard into Catalan, Finnish, French, German, Italian (in the process of being updated), Norwegian and Spanish and many more are in progress.

RDA incorporates FRBR, FRAD, ICP and now IFLA LRM. RDA presents itself as the international standard for description and access to resources designed for the digital world. It goes beyond previous cataloguing codes as it is no longer presented as a set of standards, but rather as guidelines, continuously developed and updated instructions allowing for greater flexibility of use.

RDA constitutes a content standard, not a visualisation standard. This implies a clear separation between the instructions dealing with content – with data – and those dealing with its representation. This ensures applicability in different technological contexts as long as the agencies involved in the production of the data use the same standards and the same controlled vocabulary of reference.

The first edition of the text presented a structure that clearly distinguished the two functions: to *identify* and to *connect* entities. After an introductory chapter, the first part was dedicated to the identification of entities by recording their attributes; the second part to the recording of relationships between entities. This was followed by 13 appendices (A. Capitalisation, B Abbreviations and symbols, C Initial articles, D Registration syntax for descriptive data, etc.) and the *Glossary*. The standard representation of a resource disappears in favour of a customised and contextualised description. This is a concrete result of the requirements for freedom of presentation, based on the principle of user-centricity, a concept introduced by Ranganathan in several of his works and reiterated in ICP.

The second edition of the *Toolkit* and, consequently, of the RDA text was approved in December 2020 at the end of a long process of alignment with IFLA LRM begun in 2018 as part of the RDA Toolkit Restructure and Redesign (3R) Project. It is markedly different in the way it is used and deployed. It moves from:

• an FRBR-based facility to a new structure based on IFLA LRM
• a division into sections and chapters to navigation by entity, with the help of specific guides and cataloguing policies.

Furthermore, in the transition from the first to the second edition of the guidelines, important changes were introduced in the way data are recorded and resources are described. Data can be registered in four ways:

1 through a composite, unstructured description
2 through a structured description
3 through an identifier
4 through the International Resource Identifier (IRI).

The latter mode, in particular, supports applications of the Semantic Web and linked open data. The description of resources in the first edition of the guidelines provided a set of essential elements identifying the various entities, which had to be present at all times, if applicable, in order to consider a description compliant with the standard. They were identified on the basis of their ability to:

- *identify* and *select* a manifestation
- *identify* the works and expressions contained in a manifestation
- *identify* the creator of a work
- *find* a person, corporate body or family associated with a resource.

The essential elements to describe a manifestation, for example, are:

- Title
  - Title proper
- Statement of responsibility
  - Statement of responsibility relating to title proper (if more than one, only the first recorded is required)
- Edition statement
  - Designation of edition
  - Designation of named revision of edition
- Numbering of serials
  - Numeric and/or alphabetic designation of first issue or part of sequence (for first or only sequence)
  - Chronological designation of first issue or part of sequence (for first or only sequence)
  - Numeric and/or alphabetic designation of last issue or part of sequence (for last or only sequence)
  - Chronological designation of last issue or part of sequence (for last or only sequence)
- Production statement
  - Date of production (for a resource in an unpublished form)
- Publication statement
  - Place of publication (if more than one, only the first recorded is required)
  - Publisher's name (if more than one, only the first recorded is required)
  - Date of publication
- Series statement
  - Title proper of series
  - Numbering within series
  - Title proper of subseries
  - Numbering within subseries

- Identifier for manifestation
  - Identifier for manifestation (if more than one, prefer an internationally recognised identifier if applicable)
- Carrier type
- Extent.

The official version of the *RDA Toolkit* recognises that certain elements must necessarily appear in the description of the resource and states that their choice must be made by the cataloguing agency producing the description: 'Decisions regarding the choice of essential elements and the cardinality of recorded elements may be indicated by the agency creating the metadata. This decision may be recorded in the toolkit as a policy, in a document issued by the agency or as an application profile.'[33] The solution emphasises the willingness to respect local traditions and practices and gives a fundamental role to *application profiles*, which become indispensable tools for cataloguing or, better, for creation of metadata, as they indicate which elements are to be included within a description, distinguishing between compulsory and optional elements and determining how data, transcription rules and reference vocabularies are to be recorded.

RDA is designed for use in a global context but, at the same time, it is flexible to include national and local options, as well as options motivated by a particular disciplinary context. Moreover, it shows great openness towards the entire bibliographic universe of recorded memory, not by limiting itself to the description of resources in libraries, but by turning its attention to all kinds of resources, including those stored in archives and museums. This is a fundamental aspect, which, however, still needs to be adequately developed, since RDA recognises that, from the reader's point of view, data produced by different institutions must be equally accessible. Hence the need for a shared standard capable of producing public and open data allowing the widest possible access and integration of data from different sources.

The German librarian Renate Behrens and the Austrian librarian Verena Schaffner summarise the innovative features of RDA, as a standard:

1 international; that is, based on shared principles and models
2 designed for ease of use and efficiency
3 independent from the technology used, but suitable for use on the web
4 applicable to any type of media and usable for producing metadata of any type of resource
5 applicable in all cultural institutions because it no longer focuses exclusively on bibliographic resources (Behrens and Schaffner, 2014).

RDA guarantees compatibility with ISBD, with MARC21 and with DUBLIN CORE, a metadata element set created by OCLC. To foster interoperability, RSC took into account ONIX and the metadata in use by publishers, archivists and museum staff, as well as, of course, the Semantic Web.

8

Subject Cataloguing (or Subject Indexing): Some Basics

Cataloguing 'as a whole' (description and access by author and subject) was discussed only in Cutter's *Rules* of 1876 (Cutter, 1876), written for a dictionary catalogue, that is, organised in a single sequence of access by author and subject. Since then, such comprehensive rules have not been conceived and 'cataloguing' has referred only to *descriptive cataloguing*, while *subject cataloguing*, or *subject indexing*, has been treated separately (Foskett, 1996). Ranganathan argued persuasively for the greater usefulness of an integrated subject-based catalogue (Ranganathan, 1964). The formulation 'descriptive cataloguing' was coined in the 1940s in the Library of Congress context when subject cataloguing was separated from other procedures.

Over the years, subject indexing has followed its own path. For many years it was marked by confrontations, even polemical ones, between the promoters of alphabetically ordered verbal subject access – subject access using words and phrases, referred to traditionally as 'subject headings' – and those of notational access organised according to bibliographic classification systems. Specific sectoral and disciplinary situations and needs, related to scientific, technical and management resources and documentation in the academic field or public libraries, have required or favoured the creation and development of different systems of verbal and systematic indexing – systematic referring to systems using notations of classification systems. These systems pay due respect to cultural and especially linguistic differences, much more significant in the semantic field than in descriptive cataloguing. This has led to an extreme fragmentation that has deterred the attempt to reach agreements on indexing principles or rules. However, there are the notable exceptions of the IFLA *Principles Underlying Subject Heading Languages (SHLs)* (Lopes and Beall, 1999) and the ISO 25964: 2011–2013 standard for thesauri), as well as the hypothesis of unified codes. This was demonstrated also by the difficulties in including the subject theme in the FR family, in IFLA LRM, in ICP and in RDA in a more substantial form than as a simple citation.

At present, references to theoretical elaborations reach in-depth levels in specialised areas where professional and disciplinary skills other than those of libraries are involved, such as in the search of knowledge organisation systems. Some of these are functional for the representation and retrieval of resources for their information value. At the global level, a few systems predominate: the DDC, Dewey Decimal Classification and secondarily the UDC, Universal Decimal Classification among classifications; LCSH, Library of Congress Subject Headings and its derivatives in other languages for verbal subjects, with a varied proliferation of other indexing languages applied on a national, local or disciplinary basis. In this situation, the imperative is *interoperability*, the opportunity to make the different indexing tools interact with each other while simultaneously making available the databases in which they are employed, with the renouncement of uniform systems and shared principles and application criteria. This important aspect of access requires a more elaborate treatment, which is beyond the scope of this book.

Afterword

by Giovanni Bergamin

On 1 October 2015, OCLC announced with a tweet the printing of the last catalogue card and informed us that the service of supplying catalogue cards to libraries – a total of about two billion – had lasted 44 years. It is just one of the many changes that have occurred in recent years in – to use an expression of Elaine Svenonius – 'the organisation of information'.

From Cataloguing to Metadata Creation is a long journey between founding principles, objectives and technological evolutions of the 'information organisation' service offered by libraries. At the end of this journey, we can identify endeavours in three directions with more awareness.

The first one concerns human–machine co-operation in the creation of metadata. Nowadays, some experiences in the adoption of technologies related to artificial intelligence (AI, also called machine learning) for subject cataloguing (or semantic indexing) are still active. We should remember that artificial intelligence is an 'algorithmic product completely lacking in flexibility' (Floridi, 2014) and that 'the effectiveness of an access system varies according to the intelligence invested in organizing information' (Elaine Svenonius). In other words, in this context, the levels of skills required by a librarian are higher and higher and it is always his or her 'intelligence' that makes the difference. The expected benefits from these ongoing experiences essentially concern the chance to expand the coverage (given the significant increase in resources that require bibliographic control) and not to reduce the costs of cataloguing. Work in libraries – and especially cataloguing – cannot be replaced by robots or unqualified professionals.

The second direction concerns the methods of publishing metadata. We shouldn't forget a critical stage of the journey: MARC. With MARC, libraries were the first sector to understand that, thanks to the intermediation of information technology, the metadata produced by a library could be reused and enjoyed in other libraries (and not only in libraries). We could say that MARC is for bibliographic information what the Semantic Web (or web of data) is for the web *tout court* (or web of documents). As we have seen, this journey also takes into account the work of libraries on the Semantic Web and linked data. In summary, we could say that the entry of bibliographic data into the web of data will still require a lot of work (if the goal is to guarantee the same diffusion that MARC has now). Among the reasons that make this transition difficult, at least two should be mentioned: there is no single starting point (MARC), but there are many implementations of MARC (MARC21 and UNIMARC are the most widespread, but there are others); there is no single end point, as BIBFRAME is certainly a fundamental reference ontology, especially for MARC21 data, but the discussion on metadata standards, data models and ontologies for bibliographic data is still ongoing.

The third direction concerns the experiences driven outside libraries that reuse and enhance the metadata produced by libraries in the authority control. Among these experiences – mentioned in another stage of this journey – the most significant is undoubtedly Wikidata. In this field, global collaboration perspectives have been opened up, going beyond the simple management of a single library or libraries' network catalogues. The Semantic Web makes it quite clear that libraries are not the only ones needing authority data (or metadata): for example, search engines are also interested in these types of metadata.

Endnotes

1   By 'resource' we mean everything that can be part of a library collection.

2   *'Push technology*, or server push, is a style of Internet-based communication where the request for a given transaction is initiated by the publisher or central server', https://en.wikipedia.org/wiki/Push_technology.

3   *The British Library's Collection Metadata Strategy*, www.bl.uk/collection-metadata/strategy-and-standards, p. 8.

4   Before Svenonius (2000), the verb *navigate* appeared in FRBR (1998), paragraph 5.1, p. 56 and the proposal to make it the fifth task was in the *Observations* of the AIB Study Group on Cataloguing (1999), sent to the IFLA Cataloguing Section: see AIB Study Group on Cataloguing (1999), Observations on Functional Requirements for Bibliographic Records: final report, *Bollettino AIB*, **39**, 3, 303–8. Svenonius was a colleague and friend of Seymour Lubetzky at UCLA (University of California, Los Angeles), where both taught and where Lubetzky continued to give lessons even after his retirement. He died just before the age of 105. See Svenonius and McGarry (2001); Gorman (2000); Connell and Maxwell (2000).

5   Tom Delsey and Barbara B. Tillett were Svenonius' students; Barbara Tillett earned a PhD at UCLA and Tom Delsey at the University of Western Ontario, Canada.

6   The students for the UCLA Master of Library and Information Science degree have nicknamed the book *The Red Devil* for the colour of the cover and the complexity of the topics covered, a reason for anxiety for passing the exam.

7   Serendipity, in fact, is to notice something that is beside the fixed gaze on one's own research path and to assume this intruding observation as a new object of serious research, finally arriving to discover something different from the starting point.

8   'Metadata idea is applied to different fields, but for libraries, it primarily conceives to book catalogue preparation' (Kalita and Deka, 2020).

9   The issue of *relevance*, established by an algorithm, opens up a complex
     and delicate discourse, as the established rules are often not really
     transparent.
10   See www.w3.org/standards/semanticweb/data.
11   An international non-governmental organisation that aims to develop the
     potential of the world wide web, see www.w3.org.
12   See: Anderson (1974); Davinson (1975). The topic of bibliographic
     control constantly recurs among IFLA initiatives; see, in particular, the
     conference Universal Bibliographic Control in the Digital Age: Golden
     Opportunity or Paradise Lost?, promoted by the Cataloguing Section,
     with the sections of Bibliography, Classification & Indexing and
     UNIMARC Strategic Programme on 18 August 2014 within the Lyon
     Congress, www.ifla.org/past-wlic/2014/ifla80/node/303.html.
13   Library of Congress Working Group on the Future of Bibliographic
     Control (2008). The publication of the document initiated a discussion
     involving many librarians; Thomas Mann's opinion was important, *'On
     the Record' but off the track: a review of the Report of The Library of
     Congress Working Group on The Future of Bibliographic Control, with a
     further examination of Library of Congress cataloging tendencies*,
     prepared for AFSCME 2910, the Library of Congress Professional Guild
     representing over 1,500 professional employees,
     https://tinyurl.com/bdhkvbe2, 14 March 2008,
     https://tinyurl.com/2udt8yyn, which was followed by interventions for
     and against. See, among others, Kiczek S. A. (2010), although this book
     does not deal with the history of cataloguing, some significant milestones
     should be mentioned, starting with the two conferences mentioned
     above, The Principles and Future of AACR and Bicentennial Conference
     on Bibliographic Control for the New Millennium. Among the most
     significant contributions is the so-called Calhoun Report (Calhoun, 2006,
     contested by many experts; see, in particular, the alternative, personal
     and unofficial point of view of the Library of Congress (Mann, 2006).
14   https://kcoyle.net/presentations/lita2011.html.
15   See https://data.bnf.fr.
16   www.ifla.org/files/assets/cataloguing/icp/icp_2016–it.pdf.
17   'The key title consists of the name of the publication and, eventually, a
     qualifier (often the place of publication) used in cases where it is
     necessary to distinguish the title of the publication from other equal'
     (Wikipedia).
18   Not yet realised.
19   www.ifla.org/files/assets/cataloguing/plans/action_plan_cataloguing_
     section2019_2021.pdf.

20 Glenn Patton, a member of the group, submitted a draft to the 2004 IFLA Congress in Buenos Aires.

21 The concept of *cardinality* is already present, even though not explicitly, in FRBR through the relationships represented with 1 or 2 arrows: cf. FRBR 1998, p. 13.

22 Updated version sent by Barbara B. Tillett.

23 https://en.wikipedia.org/wiki/Cataloging.

24 'Paratext is material that surrounds a published main text (e.g. the story, non-fiction description, poems, etc.) supplied by the authors, editors, printers, and publishers',
    Wikipedia, https://en.wikipedia.org/wiki/Paratext; see: Tanselle, G. T. (1998), *Literature and artifacts*. The Bibliographical Society of the University of Virginia.

25 https://original.rdatoolkit.org.

26 www.wikidata.org/wiki/Wikidata:WikiProject_Authority_control.

27 https://viaf.org.

28 https://isni.org.

29 'Although MARC metadata can be converted to linked data, many human-inferred relationships are left unexpressed in the new environment. It is functional, but incomplete. With each day of routine processing, libraries add to the backlog of MARC data that they will want to convert and enhance as linked data' (Schreur, 2018).

30 Library of Congress (2012): this document and model were developed under contract from the Library of Congress by a team from Zepheira composed of Eric Miller, Uche Ogbuji, Victoria Mueller and Kathy MacDougall; McCallum S. (2017); Bigelow and Samples (2020).

31 Last updated on 21 October 2021.

32 www.ifla.org/files/assets/cataloguing/isbd/isbd-cons_20110321.pdf, vii–viii.

33 https://access.rdatoolkit.org.

Bibliography

This bibliography indicates the main titles of reference. An historical overview can be found in:

Carpenter, M. and Svenonius, E. (eds) (1985) *Foundations of Cataloging: a sourcebook*, Libraries Unlimited.

Chan, L. M., Richmond, P.A. and Svenonius, E. (eds) (1985) *Theory of Subject Analysis: a sourcebook*, Libraries Unlimited.

For an update on the debate on topical issues, it is useful to see Gordon Dunsire's website, www.gordondunsire.com/presentations.htm and issues of *Cataloging & Classification Quarterly*.

Standards, bibliographic models, international documents

BIBFRAME: www.loc.gov/bibframe.

FRAD: www.ifla.org/files/assets/cataloguing/frad/frad_2013.pdf.

FRBR: www.ifla.org/files/assets/cataloguing/frbr/frbr.pdf.

FRBRoo: www.ifla.org/files/assets/cataloguing/FRBRoo/frbroo_v_2.4.pdf.

FRSAD: www.ifla.org/node/5849.

ICP 2009: www.ifla.org/files/assets/cataloguing/icp/icp_2009-en.pdf.

ICP 2016: www.ifla.org/files/assets/cataloguing/icp/icp_2016-en.pdf.

IFLA LRM: www.ifla.org/files/assets/cataloguing/frbr-lrm/ifla-lrm-august-2017_rev201712.pdf.

ISBD Consolidated Edition: www.ifla.org/files/assets/cataloguing/isbd/isbd-cons_20110321.pdf.

ISBD Update 2021 to the 2011 Consolidated Edition: https://repository.ifla.org/handle/123456789/1939.

ISO 5127: www.iso.org/standard/59743.html.

ISO 5963: www.iso.org/standard/12158.html.

Paris Principles: www.ifla.org/files/assets/cataloguing/IMEICC/IMEICC1/statement_principles_paris_1961.pdf.

RDA: https://access.rdatoolkit.org.

REICAT: www.iccu.sbn.it/export/sites/iccu/documenti/2015/
REICAT-giugno2009.pdf.

Further references

AIB Study Group on Cataloguing (1999) Observations on Functional
Requirements for Bibliographic Records: final report, *Bollettino AIB*, **39** (3),
303–8.

Alemu, G. (2022) *The Future of Enriched, Linked, Open and Filtered
Metadata: making sense of IFLA LRM, RDA, linked data and
BIBFRAME*, Facet Publishing.

Aliverti, C., Behrens, R. and Schaffner, V. (2016) RDA in Germany,
Austria, and German-speaking Switzerland: a new standard not only for
libraries, *JLIS.it*, **7** (2), 253–78.

Anderson, D. (1974) *Universal Bibliographic Control: a long term policy, a
plan for action*, Verlag Dokumentation.

Armitage, A., Cuneo, M. J., Quintana, I. and Carlson, Y. K. (2020) ISNI
and Traditional Authority Work, *JLIS.it*, **11** (1), 151–63.

Avram, H. D. (1975) *MARC: its history and implications*, Library of
Congress.

Baca, M. (ed.) (2008) *Introduction to* Metadata, 2nd edn, Getty Research
Institute.

Baker, T. (2013) Designing Data for the Open World of the Web, *JLIS.it*, **4**
(1), 63–6.

Balsamo, L. (1989) Funzione e Utilizzazioni del Censimento dei Beni
Librari, *Biblioteche Oggi*, **7** (1), 38.

Barberi, F. (1961) Repertorio Nazionale e Cataloghi di Cinquecentine,
*Annali della Scuola Speciale per Archivisti e Bibliotecari dell'Università
di Roma*, **1** (1), 212.

Bean, C. A. and Green, R. (eds) (2001) *Relationships in the Organization
of Knowledge*, Kluwer Academic Publishers.

Behrens, R. and Schaffner, V. (2014) *RDA. The implementation in
Germany, Austria and German-speaking Switzerland*. In *Faster, Smarter
and Richer: reshaping the library catalogue*, International Conference,
Rome (Italy), www.aib.it/attivita/convegni-e-seminari/fsr2014.

Bergamin, G. and Guerrini, M. (eds) with the assistance of Alpigiano, C.
(2022) *The Bibliographic Control in the Digital Ecosystem, JLIS.it*, **13**
(1), https://jlis.fupress.net/index.php/jlis/issue/view/34/2. Also
published in volume form by Associazione Italiana Biblioteche. (2022)
Edizioni Università di Macerata; Firenze University Press.

Berners-Lee, T. (1998) *What the Semantic Web can Represent*,
https://tinyurl.com/h7tjczap.

Berners-Lee, T., Hendler, J. and Lassila, O. (2001) The Semantic Web. A new form of Web content that is meaningful to computers will unleash a revolution of new possibilities, *Scientific American*, https://tinyurl.com/yckp8vwu.

Berners-Lee, T., Shadbolt, N. and Hall, W. (2006) The Semantic Web revisited, *IEEE Intelligent Systems*, **21** (3), 96–101.

Biagetti, T. (2001) *Teoria e Prassi della Catalogazione Nominale: i contributi di Panizzi, Jewett e Cutter*, Bulzoni.

Bianchini, C. (2005) *Riflessioni sull'Universo Bibliografico: funzioni, oggetti e modelli della catalogazione per autore e per titolo*, prefazione di Mauro Guerrini, Sylvestre Bonnard.

Bianchini, C. (2022) Intervista. In Guerrini, M. *Metadatazione: la catalogazione in era digitale*, Editrice Bibliografica.

Bianchini, C. and Guerrini, M. (2009) From Bibliographic Models to Cataloging Rules: remarks on FRBR, ICP, ISBD, and RDA and the relationships between them, *Cataloging & Classification Quarterly*, **47** (2), 105–24.

Bianchini, C. and Guerrini, M. (2015) A Turning Point for Catalogs: Ranganathan's possible point of view, *Cataloging & Classification Quarterly*, **53** (3–4), 341–51.

Bianchini, C. and Guerrini, M. (2018) New Terms for New Concepts: reflections about the Italian translation of RDA, *JLIS.it*, **9** (1), 1–5.

Bigelow, I. and Samples, J. (2020) ARC to BIBFRAME: converting the PCC to linked data, *Cataloging & Classification Quarterly*, **58** (3–4), 403–17.

Bourne, R. (ed.) (1992) *Seminar on Bibliographic Records: proceedings of the seminar held in Stockholm, 15–16 August 1990* and sponsored by the IFLA UBCIM Programme and the IFLA Division of Bibliographic Control, K. G. Saur.

Bowers, F. (1995) *Principles of Bibliographical Description*, Oak Knoll Press.

Broughton, V. (2006) *Essential Thesaurus Construction*, Facet Publishing.

Buizza, P. (2002) Dai Principi di Parigi a FRBR, *Bibliotime*, **5** (1), https://tinyurl.com/z68e9f4f.

Calhoun, K. (2006) *The Changing Nature of the Catalog and its Integration with Other Discovery Tools*, prepared for the Library of Congress. Final Report, www.loc.gov/catdir/calhoun-report-final.pdf.

Cerbo, M. A. (2011) Is There a Future for Library Catalogers?, *Cataloging & Classification Quarterly*, **49** (4), 323–7.

Chambers, S. (ed.) (2013) *Catalogue 2.0: the future of the library catalogue*, Facet Publishing.

Chan, L. M., Comaromi, P., Mitchell, S. and Satija, M. P. (1994) *Dewey Decimal Classification: a practical guide*, Forest Press.

Chan, L. M. and Salaba, A. (2016) *Cataloging and Classification: an introduction*, 4th edn, Rowman & Littlefield.

Chaplin, A. H. and Anderson, D. (eds) (1963) *International Conference on Cataloguing Principles. Paris, 9 October, 1961: report*, International Federation of Library Associations. New edition: IFLA International Office for UBC (1981).

Chen, P. S. (1976) The Entity Relationship Model: toward a unified view of data, *ACM Transactions on Database Systems*, **1** (1), 9–36.

Connell, T. H. and Maxwell, R. L. (eds) (2000) *The Future of Cataloging: insights from the Lubetzky Symposium*, American Library Association.

Cook, C. D. (ed.) (1982) *The Future of the Union Catalog: proceedings of the International Symposium on the Union Catalog*, University of Toronto, 21–22 May 1981. Also published in *Cataloging & Classification Quarterly*, **2** (1–2).

Coyle, K. (2007) The Library Catalog: some possible futures, *Journal of Academic Librarianship*, **33** (3), 414–16.

Coyle, K. (2013) Linked Data: an evolution, *JLIS.it*, **4** (1), 53–61.

Coyle, K. (2016) *FRBR, Before and After: a look at our bibliographic models*, American Library Association.

Creider, L. S. (2009) A Comparison of the Paris Principles and the International Cataloguing Principles, *Cataloging & Classification Quarterly*, **47** (6), 583–99.

Crocetti, L. (2014) *Le Biblioteche di Luigi Crocetti: saggi, recensioni, paperoles (1963–2007)*, Associazione Italiana Biblioteche.

Cutter, C. A. (1876) *Rules for a Dictionary Catalog*, US Government Printing Office.

Danskin, A. (2006) *Tomorrow Never Knows 1: the end of cataloguing?*, https://tinyurl.com/32jutxf3; then (2007) in *IFLA Journal*, **33** (3), 205–9.

Danskin, A. (2013) Linked and Open Data: RDA and bibliographic control, *JLIS.it*, **4** (1), 147–59.

Danskin, A. (2020) The Anglo-American Authority File: a PCC story, *Cataloging & Classification Quarterly*, **58** (1–4), 221–9.

Davinson, D. E. (1975) *Bibliographic Control*, Linnet Books.

Delsey, T. (1982) Standards and Standardization, *Cataloging & Classification Quarterly*, **2** (1–2), 69–81.

Delsey, T. (2007) *RDA Database Implementation Scenarios*, https://tinyurl.com/3axzwhue.

Delsey, T. (2016) The Making of RDA, *JLIS.it*, **7** (2), 25–47.

Dillon, M. (2000) *Metadata for Web Resources: how metadata works on the web*, Library of Congress, http://lcweb.loc.gov/catdir/bibcontrol/dillon_paper.html.

Dini, R. (1985) *Il Parente Povero della Catalogazione: la descrizione bibliografica dal Rapporto Henkle all'Incontro di Copenaghen*, Editrice Bibliografica.

Dini, R. (1991) *La Catalogazione*. In *Lineamenti di Biblioteconomia*, Carocci.

Domanovszky, Á. (1975) *Functions and Objects of Author and Title Cataloguing: a contribution to cataloguing theory*. English text: Thompson, A. (ed.), Verlag Dokumentation.

Dunsire, G. (2012a) Representing the FR Family in the Semantic Web, *Cataloging & Classification Quarterly*, **50** (5–7), 724–41.

Dunsire, G. (2012b) Linked Data, Libraries and the Semantic Web, *Library Science Talk*, https://tinyurl.com/5n7jyw4f.

Dunsire, G. (2020) Reconstructing Authorities: new approaches to the management and use of authority data. In Kati , T. and Tomaševi , N. (eds) *Mirna Willer: Festschrift*, Morepress, 81–98.

Dunsire, G. (2021) Bibliographic Control in the Fifth Information Age, *JLIS.it*, **13** (1), 25–36.

Dunsire, G., Hillmann, D. and Phipps, J. (2012) Reconsidering Universal Bibliographic Control in Light of the Semantic Web, *Journal of Library Metadata*, **12** (2–3), 164–76.

Dunsire, G. and Willer, M. (2013) *Bibliographic Information Organization in the Semantic Web*, Chandos Publishing.

Dziatzko, K. (1886) *Instruction für die Ordnung der Titel im Alphabetischen Zettelkatalog der Königlichen und Universitäts-Bibliothek zu Breslau*, Asher.

Escolano Rodrìguez, E. (2012) *ISBD en la Web Semántica*, Lectio magistralis en biblioteconomía, Casalini Libri.

Escolano Rodrìguez, E. (2013) ISBD Adaptation to SW of Bibliographic Data in Linked Data, *JLIS.it*, **4** (1), 119–37.

Escolano Rodriguez, E. (2022) The Updating of ISBD and its Transformation, *JLIS.it*, **13** (2), 1–12.

Fabian, C. (2020) Structure and Semantics, Coherence and Networks: the living bibliographic universe: reflections of a catalogue lover in honour of Mirna Willer a data scientist. In Kati , T. and Tomaševi , N. (eds) *Mirna Willer: Festschrift*, Morepress, 119–34.

Fattahi, R. (2010) *From Information to Knowledge: superworks and the challenges in the organization and representation of the bibliographic universe*, Lectio magistralis in library science, Florence, Italy, Florence University, 16 March 2010, Casalini Libri.

Floridi, L. (2014) *The Fourth Revolution: how the infosphere is reshaping human reality*, Oxford University Press.

Foskett, A. C. (1996) *The Subject Approach to Information*, Library Association Publishing.

Freedman, M. J. and Malinconico, S. M. (eds) (1979) *The Nature and Future of the Catalog: proceedings of the ALA's Information Science and Automation Division's 1975 and 1977 institutes on the catalog*, Oryx Press.

Genetasio, G. (2012) The International Cataloguing Principles and Their Future, *JLIS.it*, **3** (1), 1–18.

Genette, G. (1987) *Paratexts: thresholds of interpretation*, translated by Jane E. Lewin and foreword by Richard Macksey, Cambridge University Press. Translation of *Seuils* (1987), Editions du Seuil.

Ghiringhelli, L. and Guerrini, M. (2020) *Entities, Attributes, and Bibliographic Relationships: re-reading Barbara B. Tillett's PhD dissertation thirty years after*. In Kati , T. and Tomaševi , N. (eds) *Mirna Willer: Festschrift*, Morepress, 47–58.

Gorman, M. (1980) Principles, Rules, Standards and Applications. In Manning, R. W. (ed.), *AACR2 Seminar Papers*, Canadian Library Association.

Gorman, M. (1999) Metadata or Cataloguing? A false choice, *Journal of Internet Cataloging*, **2** (1), 5–22.

Gorman, M. (2000) *The Future of Cataloging: insights from the Lubetzky Symposium*, American Library Association.

Gorman, M. (2003) Cataloguing in an Electronic Age, *Cataloging & Classification Quarterly*, **36** (3–4), 5–17.

Gorman, M. (2014) The Origins and Making of the ISBD: a personal history, 1966–1978, *Cataloging & Classification Quarterly*, **52** (8), 821–34.

Gorman, M. (2015) *Our Enduring Values, Revisited: librarianship in an ever-changing world*, American Library Association.

Gorman, M. and Oddy, P. (1993) Bibliographic Standards and the Library of the Future, *Catalogue & Index*, **110** (1), 4–5.

Green, R. (2008) Relationships in Knowledge Organization, *Knowledge Organization*, **35**, 150–9.

Guatelli, F. (2020) FUP Scientific Cloud e l'editoria fatta da studiosi, *Società e Storia*, **167** (1), 155–64.

Guerrini, M. (1999) *Catalogazione*, Associazione italiana biblioteche.

Guerrini, M. (ed.) (2000) *FRBR Seminar: Functional Requirements for Bibliographic Records, Florence, Italy, 27–28 January 2000: proceedings*, Associazione italiana biblioteche. Tête-bêche in Italian and English.

Guerrini, M. (2008) *Principi di Catalogazione Internazionali: una piattaforma europea? Considerazioni sull'IME ICC di Francoforte e Buenos Aires: atti del convegno internazionale, Roma, Bibliocom, 51° Congresso AIB, 27 ottobre 2004*, Associazione italiana biblioteche.

Guerrini, M. (2009) In Praise of the Un-finished: the IFLA statement of International Cataloguing Principles, *Cataloging & Classification Quarterly*, **47** (8), 722–40.

Guerrini, M. (ed.) (2013) Global Interoperability and Linked Data in Libraries, Special issue, *JLIS.it*, **4** (1).

Guerrini, M. (2022) *Metadatazione: la catalogazione in era digitale*, Editrice Bibliografica.

Guerrini, M. and Genetasio, G. (2012) *I Principi Internazionali di Catalogazione (ICP): universo bibliografico e teoria catalografica all'inizio del XXI secolo*, postfazione di Attilio Mauro Caproni, Editrice Bibliografica.

Guerrini, M. and Manzoni, L. (2022) *RDA: Resource Description and Access*, Associazione italiana biblioteche.

Guerrini, M. and Possemato, T. (2015) *Linked Data per Biblioteche, Archivi e Musei*, Editrice Bibliografica.

Guerrini, M. and Sardo, L. (2018) *IFLA Library Reference Model (LRM): un modello concettuale per le biblioteche del XXI secolo*, prefazione di Maja Žumer, Editrice Bibliografica.

Guerrini, M., Weinberger, D., Weston, P. G. and Žumer, M. (2015) Old Wine, New Bottle? Principles and methods for a true innovation in LIS perspectives: the view of Marshall Breeding, *AIB Studi*, **55** (3), 385–403.

Holley, R. P. (ed.) (2007) *Cataloger, Editor, and Scholar: essays in honor of Ruth C. Carter*, Haworth Information Press.

Howarth, L. C. (2011) *From 'A Magnificent Mistake' to 'A Lively Community of Interest': Anglo-American Cataloguing Codes and the evolution of social cataloguing*, Lectio magistralis in library science, Florence, Italy, Florence University, 23 March 2011, Casalini Libri.

Howarth, L. C. (2012) FRBR and Linked Data: connecting FRBR and linked data, *Cataloging & Classification Quarterly*, **50** (5–7), 763–76.

International Federation of Library Associations and Institutions (2016) *Statement of International Cataloguing Principles. 2016 Edition*, IFLA Cataloguing Section and IFLA Meetings of Experts on an International Cataloguing Code 2016. Edition with minor revisions, 2017, by Galeffi, A. (chair), Bertolini M. V., Bothmann R. L., Escolano Rodríguez, E. and McGarry, D., https://tinyurl.com/5xznuhhv.

Jewett, C. C. (1853) *On the Construction of Catalogues of Cibraries, and Their Publication by Means of Separate, Stereotyped Titles, with Rules and Examples*, Smithsonian Institution.

Joudrey, D. N., Taylor, A. G. and Miller, D. P. (2015) *Introduction to Cataloging and Classification*, Libraries Unlimited.

Joudrey, D. N. and Taylor, A. G. (2017) *The Organization of Information*, Libraries Unlimited.

Kalita, D. and Deka D. (2020) Searching the Great Metadata Timeline: a review of library metadata standards from linear cataloguing rules to ontology inspired metadata standards, *Library Hi Tech*, **39** (1), 190–204.

Kempf, K. (2013) Collection Development in the Digital Age, *JLIS.it*, **4** (2), 267–73.

Kiczek, S. A. (2010) Thomas Mann's Contributions to Current Library Debates on Cataloging and Bibliographic Control, *Cataloging & Classification Quarterly*, **48** (5), 450–71.

Kumar, K. (1988) *Theory of Classification*, Vikas Publishing House.

Le Boeuf, P. (2009) *De FRBRer à FRBRoo*, Lectio magistralis in library science, Florence, Italy, Florence University, 17 March 2009, Casalini Libri.

Leavis, F. R. (1948) *The Great Tradition: George Eliot, Henry James, Joseph Conrad*, Chatto & Windus.

Library of Congress (2012) *Bibliographic Framework as a Web of Data: linked data model and supporting services*, https://tinyurl.com/mvxsa4nt.

Library of Congress, Descriptive Cataloging Division (1949) *Rules for Descriptive Cataloging in the Library of Congress*.

Library of Congress, Director of the Processing Department (1946) *Studies of Descriptive Cataloging: a report to the Librarian of Congress*, US Government Printing Office.

Library of Congress, Information Systems Office (1968) *MARC Pilot Project: final report on a project sponsored by the Council on Library Resources, Inc.*, prepared by H. D. Avram, Information Systems Office, Project director, Library of Congress.

Library of Congress Working Group on the Future of Bibliographic Control (2008) *On the Record*, https://tinyurl.com/bdhkvbe2.

Long, K. (2016) *An Entirely Too Brief History of Library Metadata and a Peek at the Future, Too*, https://tinyurl.com/3najn4x3.

Lopes, M. I. and Beall, J. (eds) (1999) *Principles Underlying Subject Heading Languages (SHLs)*, approved by the Standing Committee of the IFLA Section on Classification and Indexing. International

Federation of Library Associations and Institutions. Working Group on Principles Underlying Subject Heading Languages, De Gruyter Saur.

Lubetzky, S. (1960) *Code of Cataloging Rules: author and title entry: an unfinished draft for a new edition of cataloging rules*, American Library Association.

Lubetzky, S. (1969) *Principles of Cataloging: final report*, Phase I: Descriptive Cataloging, University of California, Institute of Library Research.

McCallum, S. (2016) *Linked Data for Cultural Heritage*, American Library Association.

McCallum, S. (2017) BIBFRAME Development, *JLIS.it*, 8 (3), 71–85.

Machetti, C. (2016) Biblioteche e Discovery Tool: il caso OneSearch e l'ateneo di Siena, *AIB Studi*, 56 (3), 391–408.

Malmsten, M. (2012) Cataloguing in the Open: the disintegration and distribution of the record, *JLIS.it*, 4 (1), 417–23.

Mann, T. (2006) *The Changing Nature of the Catalog and its Integration with Other Discovery Tools: final report, 17 March 2006, prepared for the Library of Congress by Karen Calhoun: a critical review*, www.guild2910.org.

Mann, T. (2008) *'On the Record' but Off the Track: a review of the Report of The Library of Congress Working Group on The Future of Bibliographic Control, with a further examination of Library of Congress cataloging tendencies*, https://tinyurl.com/2udt8yyn.

Maunsell, A. (1595) *The Catalogue of English Printed Books*, ed. John Windet, Facsimile Edition (1965), Farnborough, Gregg, in association with Archive P.

Miller, S. J. (2022) *Metadata for Digital Collections*, 2nd edn, Facet Publishing.

Morse, T. (2012) Mapping Relationships: examining bibliographic relationships in sheet maps from Tillett to RDA, *Cataloging & Classification Quarterly*, 50 (4), 225–48.

Murray, R. J. and Tillett, B. B.(2011) Cataloging Theory in Search of Graph Theory and Other Ivory Towers, *Information Technology and Libraries*, 30 (4), 170–84.

Nunberg, G. (ed.) (2006) *The Future of the Book*, with an afterword by Eco, U., University of California Press.

Oddy, P. (1996) *Future Libraries, Future Catalogues*, Library Association Publishing.

Online Computer Library Centre (2022) *Best Practices for Creating Sharable Metadata*, tinyurl.com/mthhzhm8.

Osborn, A. D. (1941) The Crisis in Cataloging, *The Library Quarterly*, **11** (4), 393–411.

Pisanski, J. and Žumer, M. (2010) Mental Models of the Bibliographic Universe. Part 1: Mental Models of Descriptions; Part 2: Comparison Task and Conclusions, *Journal of Documentation*, **66** (5), 643–67; 668–80.

Possemato, T. (2022) Intervista. In Guerrini, M. *Metadatazione: la catalogazione in era digitale*, Editrice Bibliografica.

Ranganathan, S. R. (1955) *Heading and Canons*, S. Viswanathan.

Ranganathan, S. R. (1961) *Reference Service*, Sarada Ranganathan Endowment for Library Science.

Ranganathan, S. R. (1964) *Classified Catalogue Code, with Additional Rules of Dictionary Catalogue Code*, assisted by Neelameghan, A., 5th edn, Asia Publishing House.

Revelli, C. (2004) La Mattanza dei Catalogatori: una funzione che rischia la dequalificazione, *Biblioteche Oggi*, **22** (5), 7–15.

Revelli, C. (2014) Carlo Revelli – Testimony. In *Faster, Smarter and Richer: reshaping the library catalogue*, International Conference, Rome, Italy, 27–28 February 2014, https://tinyurl.com/rk7h6mnb.

Riva, P. (2013) FRBR Review Group Initiatives and the World of Linked Data, *JLIS.it*, **4** (1), 105–17.

Riva, P. (2016) Il Nuovo Modello Concettuale dell'Universo Bibliografico: FRBR Library Reference Model, *AIB Studi*, **56** (2), 265–75.

Riva, P. (2018) *The IFLA Library Reference Model*, lectio magistralis in library science, Casalini Libri.

Sandberg-Fox, A. M. (ed.) (2001) *Proceedings of the Bicentennial Conference on Bibliographic Control for the New Millennium: confronting the challenges of networked resources and the web*, Library of Congress, Cataloging Distribution Service, www.loc.gov/catdir/bibcontrol.

Sardo, L. (2017) *La Catalogazione: storia, tendenze, problemi aperti*, Editrice Bibliografica.

Sardo, L. (2019) Ethics and Cataloguing, *JLIS.it*, **10** (3), 1–17.

Schreur P. (2018) RDA, Linked Data, and the End of Average, *JLIS.it*, **9** (1), 120–7.

Schreur, P. (2020) The Use of Linked Data and Artificial Intelligence as Key Elements in the Transformation of Technical Services, *Cataloging & Classification Quarterly*, **58** (5), 473–85.

Schreur, P. and Possemato, T. (2019) Authify: the reconciliation of entities at scale, paper given at the12th International Conference on Metadata and Semantics Research Communications in Computer and Information. In *Metadata and Semantic Research*, Springer.

Si, L., Zhuang, X., Xing, W. and Guo, W. (2013) The Cultivation of Scientific Data Specialists: development of LIS education oriented to e-science service requirements, *Library Hi Tech*, **31** (4), 700–24, https://doi.org/10.1108/LHT-06-2013-0070.

Sicilia, M. A., Lytras, M. D. and Miller, S. J. (eds) (2009) *Metadata and Semantics*, Springer.

Sleeman, W. and Bluh, P. (eds) (2005) From Catalog *to Gateway: charting a course for future access: briefings from the ALCTS Catalog Form and Function Committee*, American Library Association.

Smiraglia, R. P. (1992) *Authority Control and the Extent of Derivative Bibliographic Relationships*, PhD. dissertation, University of Chicago.

Smiraglia, R. P. (2001) *The Nature of a Work: implications for the organization of knowledge*, Scarecrow, 2001.

Smiraglia, R. P. (ed.) (2005) *Metadata: a cataloger's primer*, Haworth Information Press.

Smiraglia, R. P. (ed.) (2011) *Works as Entities for Information Retrieval*, Routledge.

Smiraglia, R. P. (2018) Work. In *ISKO Encyclopedia of Knowledge Organization (IEKO)*, Version 1.0; published 18 September 2018, last edited 5 February 2019, www.isko.org/cyclo/work.

Solimine, G. (1995) *Controllo Bibliografico Universale*, Associazione italiana biblioteche.

Spitzer, M. (2012) *Digitale Demenz: wie wir uns und unsere Kinder um den Verstand bringen*, Droemer.

Svenonius, E. (ed.) (1989) *Conceptual Foundations of Descriptive Cataloging*, Academic Press.

Svenonius, E. (2000) *The Intellectual Foundation of Information Organization*, MIT Press.

Svenonius, E. and McGarry, D. (eds) (2001) *Seymour Lubetzky: writings on the classical art of cataloging*, Libraries Unlimited.

Tanselle, G. T. (1987) *A Sample Bibliographical Description with Commentary*, University Press of Virginia.

Tanselle, G. T. (1998) *Literature and Artifacts*, Bibliographical Society of the University of Virginia.

Tanselle, G. T. (2020) *Descriptive Bibliography*, Bibliographical Society of the University of Virginia.

Taylor, A. G. (1988) *Cataloging with Copy: a decision-maker's handbook*, 2nd edn, with the assistance of O'Neil, R. M., Libraries Unlimited. (1st edn 1976).

Taylor, A. G. (1993) Cataloguing. In Wedgeworth, R. (ed.), *World Encyclopedia of Library and Information Services*, American Library Association, 177–81.

Taylor, A. G. (2007) *Understanding FRBR: what it is and how it will affect our retrieval tools*, Libraries Unlimited.

Taylor, A. G. and Tillett, B. B. (eds) with the assistance of Guerrini, M. and Baca, M. (2004) *Authority Control in Organizing and Accessing Information: definition and international experience*, Haworth Information Press. Also issued as *Cataloging & Classification Quarterly*, **38** (3–4) and **39** (1–2).

Tennant, R. (2002) MARC Must Die, *Library Journal*, **127** (17), 26–8.

Tennant, R. (2004) Bibliographic Metadata Infrastructure for the 21st Century, *Library Hi Tech*, **22** (2), 175–81.

Tennant, R. (2017) *'MARC must die' 15 years on*, https://hangingtogether.org/?p=6221.

Tillett, B. B. (1987) *Bibliographic Relationships: toward a conceptual structure of bibliographic information used in cataloguing*, PhD. dissertation, University of California.

Tillett, B. B. (1988) Bibliographic relationships, *International Cataloguing and Bibliographic Control*, **17** (1), 3–6.

Tillett, B. B. (ed.) (1989a) *Authority control in the online environment: considerations and practices*, Haworth Press.

Tillett, B.B. (ed.) (1989b) *Authority Control: concepts and considerations in the online environment*, Haworth Press. Also published in *Cataloging & Classification Quarterly*, **9** (3).

Tillett, B. B. (1991a) A Summary of the Treatment of Bibliographic Relationships in Cataloging Rules, *Library Resources & Technical Services*, **35** (4), 393–405.

Tillett, B. B. (1991b) A Taxonomy of Bibliographic Relationships, *Library Resources & Technical Services*, **35** (2), 150–8.

Tillett, B. B. (1993) Catalog It Once For All: a history of cooperative cataloging in the United States prior to 1967 (before MARC), *Cataloging & Classification Quarterly*, **17** (3–4), 3–38.

Tillett, B. B. (1995) Cataloguing Rules and Conceptual Models for the Electronic Environment, Keynote address, *Cataloging Australia*, **21** (3–4), 67–103.

Tillett, B. B. (2005) FRBR and Cataloging for the Future, *Cataloging & Classification Quarterly*, **39** (3–4), 197–205.

Tillett, B. B. (2008) *The Bibliographic Universe and the New IFLA Cataloging Principles*, Lectio magistralis in library science, Florence, Italy, Florence University, 14 March 2008, Casalini Libri.

Tillett, B. B. (2016) RDA, or, the Long Journey of the Catalog to the Digital Age, *JLIS.it*, **7** (2), 7–24.

Tillett, B. B. and Cristán, A. L. (eds) (2009) *IFLA Cataloguing Principles: the Statement of International Cataloguing Principles (ICP) and its Glossary: in 20 languages*, International Federation of Library Associations and Institutions, K. G. Saur.

Trombone, A. (2014) New Display Models of Bibliographic Data and Resources: cataloguing/resource description and search results, *JLIS.it*, **5** (2), 19–32.

Turbanti, S. (2021) Henriette Davidson Avram: il valore dello scambio, *Bibliologia*, **16** (21).

Taylor, A. G. (ed.) (2007) *Understanding FRBR: what it is and how it will affect our retrieval tools*, Libraries Unlimited.

Verona, E. (1959) Literary Unit versus Bibliographical Unit, *Books*, **9**, 79–104.

Weihs, J. (ed.) (1998) *The Principles and Future of AACR: proceedings of the International Conference on the Principles and Future Development of AACR, Toronto, Ontario, Canada, 23–25 October 1997*, Canadian Library Association; American Library Association.

Willer, M., Dunsire G. and Bosan i B. (2010) ISBD and the Semantic Web, *JLIS.it*, **1** (2), 213–36.

Yee, M. M. (1994) What is a Work? [1], *Cataloging & Classification Quarterly*, **19** (1), 9–28.

Yee, M. M. (1995) What is a Work? [2], *Cataloging & Classification Quarterly*, **19** (2), 5–22; **20** (1), 25–46; **20** (2), 3–24.

Yee, M. M. and Layne, S. S. (1998) *Improving Online Public Access Catalogs*, American Library Association.

Zeng, M. L. and Qin, J. (2022) *Metadata*, 3rd edn, Facet Publishing.

Žumer, M. (ed.) (2009) *National Bibliographies in the Digital Age: guidance and new directions*, International Federation of Library Associations and Institutions, Working Group on Guidelines for National Bibliographies, K. G. Saur.

Index